THE
SIX
THOUSAND
MILE
JOURNEY

Rhoda Samuels Nichter

ISBN: 978-1-6847-1365-3 (sc)
ISBN: 978-1-6847-1364-6 (e)

Lulu Publishing Services rev. date: 01/13/2020

CONTENTS

FOREWORD

"THERE WILL COME A time here in Brooklyn and all over America when nothing will be of more importance than authentic reminiscences of the past".
Walt Whitman

"When I read a book, whether wise or silly, it seems to me to be alive and talking to me".
Jonathan Swift

In this book, these "authentic reminiscences of the past" are told in a conversational tone in the hope that they will "seem to be alive and talking to you".
Rhoda S. Nichter

You will be enthralled, educated and surprised at what this book contains.

Now, as a nonagenarian, I am the youngest and last survivor of my parents' six children.

I have compiled memories of stories my parents told us as well as my own personal memories from the time I was four years old.

Some of these are revelations that were not meant to be told, and I did not reveal them for all of my 90+ years. I was "a little pitcher with big ears" or "a fly on the wall" who quietly observed and listened but never repeated what I heard. Those people are long gone and I am now telling all that I saw and heard and overheard.

These are real life stories that will give you a glimpse into life in late 1800's Europe, how the wise village rabbi was the authority for everything including treating illness, how my parent's love at first sight became a long distance love affair, making a "perena", crossing the Atlantic, food they ate in steerage, entering America, why we are not called Smith, life on the Lower East Side, bearing, raising and educating six children in the 1920's, 30's and 40's.

These nostalgic memories are a true history of surviving the Great Depression, surviving hot summers in the city, making wine at home during Prohibition, our WWII family hero, graduating from an icebox to ice cubes, graduating from a cold water flat to indoor heating.

Each chapter tells a story in a conversational tone that can stand on its own.

I surprised myself at what I had stored in my brain and remembered from almost 90 years ago, and am now telling all.

1

FAMILY BACKGROUND OF JOSEPH AND CELIA (TZIPORAH) SAMUELS

Both my parents were born in Romania. Their forbears had left Austro-Hungary to escape anti-Semitism. They settled in Romania, which reputedly, had more religious tolerance.

Hirsh Halevy Smilovici (pronounced Shmilovich and means son of Samuel) and Baruch Halevy Smilovici were brothers.

Joseph (my father) was the son of Hirsh; Tzipra (my mother) was the daughter of his brother Baruch; which made my parents first cousins.

Contrary to the dire warnings of first cousins marrying and having defective children, my parents had six normal children. I attribute this to the fact that they had totally different gene pools. My father was dark with dark brown eyes and black hair and my mother was fair with blonde hair and blue eyes

The Smilovici men all had Halevy added to their first names which means that they belonged to the Levite Tribe as opposed to the Kohanim or Israelite Tribes.

RE: FAMILY PHOTOGRAPHS

Nobody owned a camera in those days, so just before each Rosh Hashonah (Jewish New Year), Tzipra would dress up all the children and have a family picture taken by a professional photographer in his studio. I have included some of these photographs in this book, including the one on the cover, courtesy of my granddaughter, Emily H. Morris.

2

MY FATHER, JOSEPH (YUSSEL: NICKNAME)

Joseph was eighteen years old in 1899 when a neighbor came running into his house in the city of Berlad to warn him that the army recruiters were in the neighborhood to conscript all eligible men for the army. Joseph did not want to go into the Romanian army because he knew that "they treated the horses better than Jews". He ran out of the house into a neighbor's house where he hid in the coal bin until the recruiters left.

He could not go home because, if caught, he would be arrested or shot for evading the draft. He walked, hitched rides and worked his way (1,986 miles) to Hamburg, Germany. He had to make enough money to pay for the ticket on a ship.

THIS WAS THE FIRST LEG OF HIS 6,000 MILE
JOURNEY FROM ROMANIA TO AMERICA.

In Hamburg, he got on a steamboat. He had
just enough money for a ticket in steerage for the
twelve-day trip.

Steerage was in the lowest part of the ship
next to the very noisy mechanism that steered
the ship forward.

In 1900, he arrived on Ellis Island, the
entryway to the "Goldene Medina" (the Golden
Land). A translator accompanied him to an official
to register his entry. The official had trouble
with Joseph's surname "Smilovici" (pronounced
Shmilovich)). When the translator told him that
his occupation was a tinsmith/roofer, the official
responded, "Since you are a tinsmith, we will call
you "'Smith".

This explains why there are so many Smiths
in this country. Goldsmiths, silversmiths,
coppersmiths, blacksmiths, and tinsmiths all
became simply Smith when they arrived on our
shores. Joseph refused to have his name changed,
"I am not Smith. I am Smilovici (it means son of
Samuel)".

The official relented and anglicized Smilovici
to "Samlowitz", which became the family name
and eventually became "Samuels".

When Joseph arrived in New York City, three friends from the old country, who had already been here for a while, took him under their wings.

Yankel owned a Romanian restaurant on Delancy Street on the Lower East Side. Avram was an undertaker. The third was Yussel der Longer to differentiate him from my father who was also Yussel (a nickname for Joseph). Yussel der Longer was very tall, thus "der Longer". He sold diamond, gold and platinum jewelry from his pockets on a corner of Delancy Street, as he had no place of business. The jewelry was sold on trust, by giving it to the buyer to show to his wife or girlfriend, and then the buyer would either pay for it or return it. No deposit or any money exchanged hands until the sale was finalized.

Yankel told him he could eat in his restaurant free of charge. Avram, the undertaker, immediately gave him a job as a "shomer", who is a watcher for sitting "shmira" (a Jewish ritual to keep watch over the dead, who must not be left alone from the moment of passing until burial). The shomer is supposed to pray and recite psalms 24 hours a day.

Years later, Pop chuckled and had us in stitches when he told us how his three buddies did not want him to be lonely while sitting "shmira".

At 2 AM on the first night of his job, all three buddies showed up with overstuffed pastrami sandwiches plus beer and wine from Yankel's restaurant. They closed the casket, set the food out on top of it and had a jolly good picnic. After they ate, Yankel whipped out a deck of cards and all three buddies kept him company all night playing pinochle on top of the casket.

My mom warned me that Romanian men had a reputation for liking wine, women, song and gambling.

Very soon, Joseph got a job as a tinsmith for $2 a week. He installed roofs on buildings. He also made decorative pressed tin ceilings and fancy cornices which were used as ornaments over the entryways of many buildings on the Lower East Side. Some might still be there on historically preserved buildings in New York City. Antique dealers and collectors value these tin ornaments very highly today.

Before long, he started his own roofing and tinsmith business.

A ticket for passage in steerage on a steamship at that time was about $30. He saved his money and in less than four years, he was able to send for his beloved Tzipra to come to America and marry him.

3

COMPULSORY EDUCATION
IN ROMANIA

Romania had compulsory education. Jews were allowed to attend school until the equivalent of our sixth grade. Joseph lived in Berlad, a small city. He was a very good student. He could add long columns of numbers in his head and come up with the correct answer. Jews were not allowed to enter the professions. Instead, at the age of thirteen, boys were apprenticed to the trades. Thus, my father became a tinsmith/roofer and Shmiel, the middle brother became a carpenter. Usher, the oldest brother worked and learned the business in their father's "kretchma" (bar/restaurant).

The big plus in learning to read and write Romanian was that it is a romance language, which has the same alphabet as English. When my parents came to America, they were able to read and write and just had to learn the language, which they did very quickly. In countries adjacent to Romania: Russia, Poland, Greece, most people were illiterate. Those countries use the Cyrillic (Slavic) alphabet. They did not know how to sign their names and signed the proverbial "X" when asked to sign. You had to be wealthy and of a certain social and religious class to attend school. The numerals for both alphabets were Arabic, which we use today. The upper classes in those countries kept the peasants uneducated and illiterate because it suited their economy.

All Jewish children attended "cheder" (Hebrew School), where they learned to read and write Hebrew, study Torah (the first five books of the Jewish Bible). The boys were Bar Mitzvahed at the age of thirteen. Bar Mitzvah means Son of the Commandments and symbolizes coming of age and being accountable for their actions.

Tzipra attended the only school in her village, which was in a convent where the teachers were nuns. The nuns renamed Tziporah's biblical name with the heavenly name "Celia". Although the nuns were very kind, if she tried to write with her left hand because she was left-handed. They would hit her hand with a ruler. As a result, she wrote and cut with her right hand and did everything else with her left.

4

MY MOTHER, TZIPRA
(SHORT FOR TZIPORAH)

My mother Tzipra was born in 1888 on the day after Purim (a holiday that celebrates the downfall of Haman, a tyrant). Many European Jews did not know their actual date of birth. Instead, their birthdays were associated with a holiday. My father was born in 1882 on Rosh Hashonah (Jewish New Year).

Falciu, (pronounced Falchoo) was the very small village where my mom was born. Her humorous observation was that Falciu sounded like a sneeze. If you sneezed upon entering the village, by the time you wiped your nose, you were out of town.

Her father managed the estate of a "poretz" (a wealthy landowner). Her mother's name was

Feigele (which means "little bird") which explains why some women are called "Birdie".

Feigele died during a cholera epidemic when my mom was three years old. At the time, they did not know that cholera spread by contaminated drinking water and lack of sewage treatment. The symptoms of cholera are severe diarrhea and dehydration. The treatments today are antibiotics, hydration and replacement of salts and sugars lost by the victim. Cholera victims were isolated and most of them died. My mom remembered visiting her sick mother where everything was white. Her mother was covered in a white blanket in a white tent in a field hospital set up for the overwhelming number of cholera victims. That was the last time she saw her mother. Today, modern sewage and water treatment has effectively eliminated cholera in most countries.

Falciu was on the edge of the Prut River bordering Bessarabia, which belonged to Russia at the time and patrolled by rifle-carrying Russian soldiers. Mom told stories about how she and her little friends would tease and taunt the soldiers on the other side of the river, who would then playfully point their guns at the girls, who would run away screaming and laughing.

One evening in the early 1930's, as was our custom, all of us, which included Mom, Pop, my siblings: Harry, (a very young doctor), Max (a pharmacy school student), Sam (an accounting school student) and the three youngest children: Florence, Barney and I, were sitting around after Friday night dinner, chatting, noshing on fruit and cracking walnuts and almonds with a nutcracker.

We listened, with great interest as my mother told us the story of how a Russian rabbi cured her of a painful illness when she was about four years old. She had such severe pains in her belly for a few days that she moaned and cried. Since there was no doctor in her small village, her father took her to the village rabbi to see if he could help her. The rabbi listened very carefully to her and her father and this is what he advised, "There is a certain rabbi in Russia who has medical knowledge. Take the child across the border, find him and see if he can help her."

Her father wrapped her in blankets and took the horse and buggy on to the barge, which took them across the Prut River into Russia to find the rabbi.

When they found him, he listened to her and said "Take the child to the slaughterhouse and ask the "shochet" (Kosher ritual slaughterer) to give you the "kishkas" (intestines) of a freshly slaughtered calf. Wrap the "kishkas" around the child's body and leave them there for 24 hours."

Her father did as the rabbi instructed and headed home. Tzipra remembered that the raw kishkas smelled terrible and were slimy. But she tolerated them because the rabbi had given instructions and she was afraid to disobey him.

Twenty-four hours later, when the "kishkas" were removed, little Tzipra had recovered! The pain had disappeared!

We all turned to look at Harry. His reaction was interesting because you would expect a modern young doctor, a man of science, to pooh-pooh such a story. Instead, he speculated that "Maybe there was something in the fresh "kishkas" that modern science uses today in pharmaceuticals for stomach ailments.

Tzipra's father remarried when she was still a little girl. As was the custom in those days, he married a distant relative and had three children with her: Pessl, Bella and Moshe Aaron. My mom reminisced that although her stepmother was kind to her, she favored her own children. Even as a young child, my mom felt the difference. She vowed that she would be the best mother in the world to her own children someday.

5

TZIPRA COMES TO AMERICA

Back in Romania, fair-haired, blue-eyed Tzipra had many suitors, but even though she had seen him just once at a family wedding, when she was twelve and he was eighteen, she had handsome, dark, swarthy Joseph in her mind. It was love at first sight for both of them when he said to her at that time, "I am going to marry you some day."

She received many letters from him in America, which took weeks and months to deliver. Then one happy day in 1904, a ticket arrived in the mail. I don't know whether it was really a ticket or money. Mom always referred to it thus, "He sent me a ticket to come to America."

Tzipra was just a little past sixteen at this time. Her father found a neighbor who was traveling at the same time. He asked her to watch over

Tzipra, which she did. They traveled in a horse-drawn coach to Hamburg, Germany where they boarded a steamship called "The Patritza" with accommodations in steerage for the twelve-day trip.

Tzipra, a little past sixteen, had to lie about her age in order to travel, and was listed on the ship's manifest as being nineteen. She was kosher and would not eat the food the ship provided. The food for steerage passengers consisted of food that would not rot or get moldy for the twelve days, so they were offered very dry bread, salted or pickled herring, prunes and sometimes some kind of dried beef. However, there was always a big pot with boiled potatoes available, so she lived on boiled potatoes for the entire trip.

Her greatest worry was that she would get lice in her long, thick hair. She had heard that you would not pass the health inspection if you had lice and they would send you back "where you came from".

It was September 15, 1904 when Tzipra arrived on Ellis Island. Joseph was there to meet her, but immigration authorities would not let her go with him because they were not married and they could not be sure that he had honorable intentions. She had to stay there until he found a female relative to take care of her. Mom said she was terrified to be there overnight, afraid that nobody would come to get her. She described the bed in the women's dormitory as being very high (it was probably a double decker), and she shuddered when she described the "vantzen" (bedbugs) crawling around, to be as big as the nail on her thumb. She held up her thumb to demonstrate the size.

The next day, Joseph arrived with Mima Meltzer, her stepmother's sister, with whom she was allowed to go. Mima Meltzer, along with her husband and five children, lived in a fifth floor walkup at 82 Eldridge Street on the Lower East Side of New York City.

On the way to Mima's, they passed a pushcart selling bananas. Joseph bought a bunch and gave one to Tzipra who had never seen a banana before. When he showed her how to peel it and eat it, she fell in love with her first American food and claimed that from that moment on, bananas were her favorite food.

Back in Romania, the belief was that the higher up you lived in a building, the richer you were. Since there were no indoor toilets, Tzipra discovered the awful truth was that the outhouses (privies) were located on street level at the back of the building. You had to go down the five flights from Mima's apartment to use them.

They used chamber pots (referred to as "cockteppels") upstairs in the apartment. There was no plumbing, as we know it, no faucets, and no toilets. There was a pump next to the kitchen sink, which was pumped up and down to draw water up. The bathtub was in the kitchen where they had the proverbial Saturday bath. There were public bath houses where you could go to bathe and get hosed down by an attendant.

In the 1930's, I remember going with my mom to Silver's Baths located on the boardwalk on Coney Island, which was a public, but more private, bath house, more like a spa, where there were steam rooms and saunas and a swimming pool, and a matron who would hose you down if you requested it.

One week later, on Shabbas Bereishes (a holiday which signifies the renewal of reading the Torah after finishing it on Simchas Torah), Joseph and Tzipra were married in Mima Meltzer's apartment.

6

MARRIAGE AND FAMILY

After they were married, Joseph and Tzipra rented an apartment on Essex Street on the Lower East Side of Manhattan. Tzipra had brought her "perena" (featherbed or down quilt) as part of her trousseau.

In Romania, when their mothers bought a duck or goose for dinner, young girls started to pluck the soft feathers (down) from the ducks and geese and save them to make the perena as part of their trousseau to bring to their marriage.

For years, they worked on preparing the perena, which is practically indestructible, and lasts for a very long time. I remember the perena when I was little and my parents were married about twenty-five years at that time.

Eventually, after steam heat was introduced, and a perena was not needed on cold nights, my mom made down pillows for everyone from the original perena.

Tzipra, not quite 17, happily became pregnant almost immediately. She spoke to the baby growing in her belly every day and told him, "You will be a doctor." The hope and dream of every Jewish mother was to have a son who was a doctor. Her first son, Harry, was born in July 1905. He was a beautiful child with dark curly hair and intelligent eyes. Mom said he was the spitting image of his father, but I saw some of my mother in him.

When Harry was five years old, mom took him to be registered for kindergarten. He did not speak English because his parents spoke Yiddish most of the time, but Romanian when they did not want the children to understand what they were saying. Harry was very bright, ambidextrous and blessed with a photographic memory. He learned English very quickly, and was so brilliant that when he graduated from Boys High School, he was valedictorian. He completed pre-med and at the time around 1923, it was difficult to get into medical school because there was a quota on the number of Jewish students that would be accepted. Luckily, after sweating it out, he was accepted at Columbia Medical School. He did his internship at Beth-El Hospital (now Brookdale) on Rockaway Parkway in Brooklyn.

After the end of World War I (1918), Joseph prospered in his roofing and tinsmith business. He bought a family touring car called a "Mitchell". It had a convertible top and was considered a very classy car to own at the time. I have a Brownie snapshot of my sister Florence leaning on the Mitchell's fender.

He also bought a model T Ford which seated two and squeezed three in the front. The one in the middle had to leave room for the stick shift. The Ford had a rumble seat where the trunk is today. It seated two when opened and you had to climb on the fender to get in. You are exposed to the elements because the rumble seat had no roof. A tarpaulin was stored there to hold over your head in case of rain.

At the time, Joseph and Tzipra owned a two-family house at 89 Glenmore Avenue in the Brownsville section of Brooklyn. P.S. 84 was across the street from the house because Tzipra insisted that they live close to a school and a library. The library was on Osborne Street around the corner.

The family occupied the lower apartment. The upstairs apartment was rented to a tenant, which brought some income. Joseph had his roofing/tinsmith shop on the street level. A nearby shed had housed the horse and wagon and were replaced by the truck.

The apartments each had three bedrooms. One bedroom had a separate entrance to the hallway. When Harry entered medical school, his parents arranged with the tenant to give up that extra bedroom and that became Harry's study and laboratory.

Mom shuddered when she described going into the room to clean it and finding a human skeleton hanging there alongside a skull and jars filled with body parts preserved in formaldehyde. Harry loved studying medicine. It came to him very easily. He received his medical degree in 1926, the same year I was born.

My mother prided herself in the fact that she did not give birth to a child every ten months.

Life was good as Joseph prospered in his business. Tzipra was happily busy bearing and taking care of the children.

Unfortunately, the whole family (Joseph and all the children) were caught up in the flu epidemic of 1918. At the time, it was referred to as the "Spanish influenza" and killed 50 million people worldwide. Research today links the Spanish flu to Asian pigs and fowl. It was a virus passed by virus-infected droplets, when inhaled, attacked the lungs, often causing pneumonia, for which there was no medication. Usually, the pneumonia victim ran a high fever and had to pass a "crisis" (very high fever) to recuperate. If they did not pass the crisis, death followed.

The whole family was infected. Tzipra nursed everybody, including some of the neighbors. She would change their wet sweaty bedclothes, wash everything by hand with soap, scrub on a corrugated washboard, and then hang everything on a clothesline to dry. There were no washers and dryers in those days. They would have died if not for her care.

She was also busy making chicken soup for everybody. She did not get the flu even though she was heavily exposed to it every day. She claimed that God was watching over her so that she could help everybody.

Barney, Florence Sam, Max and Harry

7

HARRY ESTABLISHES A MEDICAL PRACTICE

At this time, Joseph contracted to put the roofs on fifty houses for a builder named Cutler. When the job was done, Cutler, like many builders then, as well as today, stiffed the individual contractors who had done work for him. Pop had paid his workers and supplied all the materials. When he presented his bill, Cutler refused to pay him the agreed-upon price, claiming that all the houses had not been sold yet and that he did not have the money to pay him.

After much arguing and haggling, Cutler agreed to let Pop have one of the houses for the down payment. There was a mortgage of $20,000 still to be paid. It was the best Pop could do, so he settled.

It was 1926 when we moved from Glenmore Avenue to the new house at 226 East 92 Street in East Flatbush. Harry had completed his internship at Beth-El Hospital and was now a practicing doctor, and I was six months old

During the years that I grew up, I would often hear my parents discussing financial problems, especially during depression days of the 1930's. They blamed "that bastard Cutler" for their money problems because "If he had paid Pop what he owed, we would be sitting pretty now".

They always referred to him as "that bastard Cutler". I grew up thinking that Cutler's first name was "bastard".

My parents kept the house on Glenmore Avenue, which now had two tenants and brought some income unless there was a repair for which the landlord was responsible. That was the first time I heard the expression, "You are better off being a rich tenant than a poor landlord."

Pop still had his tinsmith-roofing shop on the street level.

The house on 92nd Street had an ideal arrangement for Harry to establish his medical practice. There was a separate entrance from the front porch into the sun parlor, which became the waiting room for his patients. The room next to that, which would have been our living room, became his office and examining room.

He was a GP (general practitioner), which means that he did everything medical for his patients. All medical school graduates start out as GPs until they decide what, if anything, they want to specialize in.

He had a lively practice, treating neighbors and anybody who needed a doctor. Everybody was poor so he charged $2 for an office visit, and $3 for a house call. He delivered all the babies in the neighborhood. Mrs. Steiner, the plumber's wife, had a baby every year. Harry had a barter arrangement with Mr. Steiner: plumbing service in exchange for medical service.

Harry was very kind and generous and loved being a doctor.

Everybody in the neighborhood loved and respected him and the respect rubbed off on our family as well.

Mom was very proud of him and always referred to him as "my son the doctor". One anecdote had her introducing her son Sam as "my son the accountant, brother of my son the doctor".

Harry and Pop loved to go to Canarsie in Brooklyn where there were outdoor beer gardens under big spreading trees and oompah-oompah bands playing German polka music. The waiters put gigantic bowls of pretzels on the table. I would be given a cherry soda and a taste from the pitcher of beer that everybody was drinking. All the big beer companies were represented there:

Trommers, Piels, Schlitz, Anheuser Busch, and Schaefer. It was a fun place to go. I usually fell asleep in the car on the way home, and had to be carried into the house.

The outdoor beer gardens eventually closed down because bird droppings from the trees became a nuisance.

In 1929, Pop had a stroke, which paralyzed one arm and one leg and caused aphasia (loss of speech).Harry and Mom took care of him at home.

Supporting the family fell on Harry, who accepted the responsibility and became the leader and caretaker of the whole family. Max was in Columbia Pharmacy School and was not earning anything yet. Sam decided to study accounting as the shortest route to making a living. Teenagers Florence and Barney and I, a pre-schooler, were still young enough to need support. Eventually, Pop regained the use of his arm and leg, but his speech was halting.

8

RACES AND RESTAURANTS

Dr. Harry I. Samuels, my oldest brother, was a big fan of horseracing. Every chance he had, he would go to Belmont or Aqueduct racetracks.

He enjoyed the gambling, but to him, it was a science to be studied. He knew the history of all the horses and the jockeys as well. It was his hobby. The races were seasonal, so it wasn't constant.

He also enjoyed going to the Trotters at Roosevelt Raceway in Westbury on Long Island. Trotters races are also known as harness racing.

Trotters pull a two-wheeled cart (sulky) with a driver. The trotters' gait is where the horses' legs move in diagonal pairs, where the right foreleg moves forward and so does the left hind leg and vice versa.

The pacer is another horse trained for harness racing. A pacer's foreleg moves forward in unison with the hind leg on the same side.

I remember going with him to these races, as well as the dog races in Florida. Greyhounds with their lean bodies and long legs are used for dog races, where they chase a fake automatic rabbit. Mom was a great dog-lover. Therefore, Harry would take Mom and me to the fence at the starting point of the race where the dogs were lined up, and ask Mom to pick the dog she thought would win. She would pick one by "the intelligent face", and Harry would bet on that one. Sometimes she picked a winner, sometimes she did not. But it was fun anyhow.

When he was still married to Hattie, she was never around, and after they were divorced, she was still not around, so we had the pleasure of spending time with him. He was much loved by all of us.

When Harry came home from the track, we would ask him how he made out. If he won, he would say so, if not, he would always say, "broke even" as he put it. He never lost.

With his photographic memory, he knew a lot about everything and was happy to impart the information to whoever was with him. Any time we went to a party or gathering of any sort, if you saw a cluster of people listening, enraptured by someone, Harry was holding court. He had a big personality and was always a welcome guest.

Going to a restaurant with him was always fun and an adventure. Mom was kosher, so he would find some wonderful restaurants that served fish she would eat. Of course, his favorite was Lundy's in Sheepshead Bay, Brooklyn. It was a gigantic old cavernous restaurant carefully overseen by a big black maitre d', who ran the place like an old plantation, with black waiters who quivered and quaked when he gave them a look or an order. He loved Harry, who was a frequent patron. When he saw Harry come in, he would give him a jovial greeting and order the waiters to take good care of him. I am sure Harry tipped him generously. Sometimes, Harry went there alone, and other times, he would have the whole family as his guests.

The food was always excellent at Lundy's.We would start with clam chowder or shrimp cocktail. Mom laughingly and good-naturedly referred to shrimp as "kleine veremlach" (little worms). If somebody ordered lobster, Mom described it as "a groisse cockroach" (a large cockroach). These were shellfish, which were not kosher. Believe me; it did not turn us off on eating the shrimp and lobster. We thought she was funny. In order to be kosher, fish had to have scales. She ordered the filet of sole, which was always excellent. Dessert was always blueberry pie topped with ice cream.

Another unforgettable restaurant that he frequented was Richie Nicolello's near the clock tower in Roslyn, Long Island. Harry introduced me to my first taste of shrimp here. When Richie heard that I had never had shrimp before, he prepared shrimp marinara for me himself. I never forgot the taste of that shrimp, and became a fan of shrimp marinara to this day.

The whole family of Dubrow's Cafeteria on Eastern Parkway near Utica Avenue were Harry's patients. We were always treated royally when we went there. The owners of "Famous" dairy restaurant opposite Dubrow's were also his patients. These were great places to eat, and I remember them well. My mom did a lot of cooking in between these outings to restaurants.

Another of Harry's patients that I remember are the Rudutsky family, manufacturers of "halvah", a middle and eastern European confection made of sesame seeds and tahini. They were known as the "Halvah Kings."

One of his patients, a children's dress manufacturer, learned that Harry had a little sister. He gave him many dresses for me, which were samples that they would not sell anyhow. I was very well dressed for school at that time.

9

HARRY'S MARRIAGE

It was 1930, just after the stock market crash of 1929. What follows are the observations and memories of a four or five year-old, who was a little pitcher with big ears. You won't hear much about Pop, my father, because he had had a stroke in 1929 and was left with aphasia (halting speech). He didn't say much.

Harry was a young doctor. The economy was in the dumps. People had no money. Harry was the main financial support for the family.

He came home one day and announced that he had met this beautiful redheaded girl, that they were in love, and wanted the family, especially Mom, to meet her and hopefully approve. They had been introduced by a "shadchen" (matchmaker) hired by her father.

Her parents, Jacob and Minnie Hoffman, had been Russian immigrants. Neither one of them could read, having come from Russia, where there was no education for most people. They signed "X" when a signature was required. But Mr. Hoffman did not let that hold him back. He managed to become a partner in Knoxall Dresses, a dress manufacturing company in the garment center in New York City. He became very wealthy, in spite of the rest of the country's deep depression.

He bought a home in a very lovely section of Flatbush, furnished it with expensive furniture and hired many servants, which Minnie knew how to order around.

Minnie was barely five feet tall. Jacob was much taller. They were matched by a "shadchen" (matchmaker) in Russia. He could not make conversation, unless he was talking about his business. He was wise enough to instruct the current "shadchen" that he wanted professional husbands for his daughters. And that he would provide a large cash dowry when they were married.

Mom invited the girl, Hattie, for Friday night dinner so the family could meet her. When she walked in the front door, we saw this gorgeous redhead, dressed very elegantly, carrying a beautiful bouquet of flowers for Mom. Mom served dinner. Hattie was very complimentary and was quick to help with clearing dishes. She seemed very nice.

After dinner, Harry took her home. When he returned, he wanted to know what we, especially Mom, thought of her. Mom was concerned that she looked like she had expensive tastes. Could Harry afford to keep her in the style she was accustomed to and still help the family? That was when he disclosed that Mr. Hoffman had promised a large dowry.

Soon afterwards, the whole family was invited to the Hoffmans for dinner. Of course, the servants did all the work, while Minnie sat, silent most of the time, except to order the servants.

In June 1931, Harry and Hattie were married at Union Temple opposite Prospect Park in Brooklyn. It was a magnificent affair— the wedding of the year. The bride had 12 bridesmaids: my sister Florence was one, her older sister Tootsie (married to Julie, a dentist) was matron of honor, Babe, (her younger sister, who eventually married a lawyer) was maid of honor, two flower girls: me with long black curls and Arlene with long blondish curls.

Mr. Hoffman's dress company had made all the dresses, including the bride's, in a beautiful eggshell color. Photographs were taken in the garden of Union Temple.

As a flower girl, I remember tossing petals from a tiny straw basket that I held as I walked down the aisle before the bride. At the age of five, I took this assignment very seriously. I was very aware of what I was doing. I didn't want to embarrass Harry or Mom by doing something foolish.

My mother, Tzipra, looked very regal. She wore all the jewelry that Pop had bought from Yussel der Longer on the corner of Delancy Street and given to her when each of her babies were born. She looked like the Queen of Romania!

Harry and Hattie went to the Pacific Northwest for their two-week honeymoon. This was unheard of because in our milieu, most people honeymooned at Niagara Falls or the Catskills, or a hotel in the city for a night or two.

When they returned, they rented two adjacent apartments on street level at 181 Rockaway Parkway, a short distance from Beth-El Hospital, where Harry performed surgery. The setup for his office practice was in one of the apartments, with living quarters in the other. It was really very nice.

I remember the apartment was furnished very tastefully with magnificent antiques carefully placed. Hattie had excellent taste, and she knew what she was doing. Little as I was, I was impressed. The apartment with the office was furnished very tastefully as well.

One day they arrived at our house on East 92nd Street in a royal blue Pierce Arrow, a luxury auto made in Buffalo. The spare tires were stored in built-in compartments on the fenders on the side of the car. It cost $8000 compared to $575 for a Model T Ford. Of course, Harry drove, but we were amazed when Hattie pulled up in front of our house. We didn't know any women who knew how to drive in those days. When they came to visit, all the neighbors would come out to admire the car.

In overheard conversation, I learned that the $10,000 dowry promised by Mr. Hoffman was spent on the car, the honeymoon and the furniture. Harry had hoped to use some of that money to take care of the family, but he did not have any choice because it was given to Hattie, who did what she pleased with it.

This was the first disappointment in the marriage. The next one occurred when a neighbor, Mrs. Weinstein, asked Mom if she knew that her new daughter-in-law had been married before. In those days, a divorced woman was looked upon as "used merchandise." Mom was shocked, and asked Harry about it. I think he was surprised too. He came back a short time later and told Mom that the marriage had been annulled.

Between the dowry reassignment and the annulment, Mom was left with a bad taste in her mouth. Her son, the doctor, her pride and joy, had made a bad marriage. There was nothing to be done. Harry claimed that he was crazy about Hattie and that it would not change anything.

Beth-El Hospital wanted to expand, so they needed fund-raising.

Hattie became involved with the Doctors' Wives Auxiliary, which held various fund-raising functions. I remember Hattie hosting elegant luncheons as fund-raisers in their apartment. She always asked me if I wanted to help, which I did. I learned a lot about hosting from observing her in action.

Mom joined the Sisterhood of Beth-El Hospital. They were older women, not necessarily affiliated to anybody at the hospital. The president of the Sisterhood, Mrs. Ida Blockoff, was very sincere in her efforts to help the hospital. It seems that the hospital had saved her life at one time. She had no children and took to me immediately. I was always there because I was very well-behaved and my mom took me everyplace with her.

My mom planned many fund-raisers. She planned theater parties where she would make arrangements with the manager of the Hopkinson Yiddish Theater or the Second Avenue Theater to get a block of seats at a discount. Then the Sisterhood would sell them at a profit and donate it to the hospital. They arranged fund-raising luncheons and parties. They raised enough money to build the Menorah Annex, a separate building to serve just women, pregnant and otherwise. As a matter of fact, Florence gave birth to her children there and I gave birth to my first child there.

Harry's practice grew and he decided to specialize in orthopedics.

After several years on Rockaway Parkway, they moved to 1688 Carroll Street just off Utica Avenue in Brooklyn because that location was more easily accessible via public transportation. There, patients could walk in to the street level office. The private living quarters were upstairs.

When Harry came to visit and check on Mom and Pop, I was usually outside in front of the house with my friends, playing potsy or "A my name is —", or skelly with checkers made out of old bottle caps or jumping rope or playing stoop ball.

Sometimes, he would give me a quarter (which was a lot of money for a kid) and he would give each of my friends a quarter as well! They were overwhelmed and could not wait to tell their moms about the gift. My friends, Rozzie, Nettie, Harriet and Paul (who played with the girls rather than the boys), used to hang around my house hoping that Harry would show up and give them another quarter. It didn't happen quite as often as they would have liked.

HATTIE

As the years passed, Hattie did not have a child. I was not privy to what that was all about.

I recall one incident from when I was about 13 or 14 years old. One Saturday afternoon, Hattie called me on the telephone and asked me if I would do her a favor. Of course, I always agreed to anything she wanted me to do. It seems that she had gone shopping early that morning at S. Klein's Department Store on Union Square (14th Street) in the city, she had bought six maternity dresses, but when she tried them on at home, she decided to return them. She asked me if I would return them for her. I went right over, picked up the dresses and took the IRT subway to 14th Street.

Returns were very easy there if the original tags were attached. I had gone with my mother many times when she returned things. I went to the return window and gave the merchandise to the clerk. She asked me to wait while she went into a back room.

A few minutes later, two big men came out and asked me to come with them. Later on, I realized that they were store detectives. I went with them, not knowing what was happening, They sat me down in an isolated room and started to question me. I was very naïve. I knew that I hadn't done anything wrong. It seems that they thought that

I had stolen the merchandise, because it was bought the same day. I was being accused of shoplifting. I explained that my sister-in-law had bought them and asked me to return them. I gave her name, telephone number, and told them that she was married to my brother who was a doctor. They called her, gave me the refund and I walked away. I was a little shaken by the incident.

Luckily, for me, Hattie was home to answer the phone or things might not have been that pleasant.

In retrospect, with maturity, I think back and wonder why she bought maternity dresses and returned them the same day. Did she think she was pregnant? Did the pregnancy end when she returned home from shopping?

We never heard that she was pregnant. Sometime later on, she did have a hysterectomy, which meant that she could not ever bear children.

This too was a great disappointment to Mom. Her son would never have children with this wife.

Hattie's sisters were procreating nicely. Tootsie had two beautiful boys: Alden and Freddy. Hattie's younger sister, Babe, married to a lawyer by now and living in New Jersey, had two children, as well.

Hattie threw herself into being active with the Doctors' Wives Auxiliary and became an officer. About that time, plastic surgery was becoming popular, so she decided to have a nose job to correct the bump in her nose. I didn't see much difference after the surgery, but she was happy with the change. When she had to provide a photograph of herself for the organization's yearbook, it was interesting that she posed showing her new profile.

She never cooked, when you opened her refrigerator, there was a can of coffee in it, that is all. She claimed that if there was food in the refrigerator, the maid would eat it all. If she was home, Harry took her out to a restaurant for dinner. If not, Harry would go to a restaurant by himself.

He was very generous with tips, and his usual restaurants would make special food for him. Mom made dinner for him frequently.

Hattie was home less and less. She would go to Florida in the winter for months at a time. Harry could not go with her, because he had his medical practice and he had to keep the money coming in.

My mother started to hear stories about Hattie with other men. She never told Harry, but he started to hear gossip as well.

To make a long story a little shorter, after twenty years of marriage, Hattie said she was getting a divorce. I do not know if Harry was sad or glad because I think he still loved her. She had taken up with an executive of Maidenform Bras. He was probably a better match for her, emanating from the women's garment center, which was more her milieu, given that her father was in the garment center. Harry was too intellectual for her. I do not know if she and Mr. Maidenform ever got married. Looking back, I think he might have been a married man.

When she left Harry, she took all the furniture, leaving the house empty except for a club chair, which had been custom-made for him.

Shortly afterward, Mom moved into the apartment to take care of him. It also saved money for Harry because Harry had been paying Mom's rent.

Mom was very angry at Hattie for treating Harry so shabbily. When Mom talked about her, she always referred to her as "die roite corva" (the redheaded whore}.

When Mom looked at their wedding pictures, she would become angrier with Hattie. One day, she took a pair of cuticle scissors and cut Hattie's face out of the photograph of the entire wedding party. She didn't want to destroy the whole thing because Florence was in it as a bridesmaid and I was in it as flower girl. The first time I saw the picture with Hattie's face cut out, I almost laughed—a wedding picture with the bride's face cut out looked comical and strange. But, of course, I understood her anger.

This woman, "die roite corva" had made a fool out of her wonderful son.

10

MAX (FAMILY HERO OF WORLD WAR II)

Max, Tzipra's second son, was born when Harry was about three years old. In her eyes, all her children were beautiful and exceptional, especially the latest one to be born, but Max was "especially beautiful".

Max was an outstanding student as well as an excellent athlete on both the football and swimming teams at Boys High in Brooklyn, which was considered an elite school at the time. For a while, he aspired to be a gym teacher but then decided to study medicine, like his brother Harry.

Unfortunately, the Great Depression of the 1930's had prevented his undertaking the many years and expense it took to become a doctor, so he took a shorter route in education by studying pharmacy at Columbia.

Upon graduation, he got a job almost immediately clerking in Dave Katz's drug store on Rockaway Parkway in Brooklyn and was able to contribute to supporting the family.

The Depression hit everybody hard. The goal in life at that time was to have enough money to feed your family and afford a place to live. I remember seeing some evicted families' furniture out in the street because they could not pay their rent.

Several years later, after he was married, Max owned a drug store on the corner of Jamaica Avenue and 111th Street in Jamaica, Queens. He was a very ethical pharmacist and would not carry any items such as toys, candy and other paraphernalia which were not pharmaceutical or related to health.

He refused to install a soda fountain, which many drug stores did in order to make a little more money. He ran a pharmacists' pharmacy, which doctors and other pharmacists greatly respected.

During World War II, childless and patriot that he was, Max did not wait to be drafted into the service. He sold his drug store, and volunteered to serve as a pharmacist on an army hospital ship in the Pacific. The job of a hospital ship was to float around in the ocean until notification that a battle was over and the wounded had to be picked up to be treated on the ship while heading for the nearest hospital, usually in Hawaii or the Philippines. Most of the wounds were burns from flame-throwers and Max had to make his own unguents to start the healing and relieve the pain.

Hospital ships were not immune from enemy bombing. Fortunately, after many harrowing experiences, Max's ship survived.

When his ship docked in Shanghai, China, he was credited with saving the lives of several hundred Jews who had fled across Siberia on foot to escape the Holocaust and were now stuck in Shanghai, most of them ill and in need of medical care.

He was searched by one of the refugees, who walked up to him as he was leaving the ship, and asked him, "Bist a Yid?" (Are you a Jew?").When Max affirmed that he was a Jew, the man asked if he would go with him to see if he could help his people somehow.

He was taken to a big barn where he found dozens upon dozens of refugees in very bad shape. They were suffering from pneumonia, heart problems, and malnourishment and foot infections because many had walked barefoot a good part of the way, having worn-out their shoes or lost them. There were some newborn babies.

He was offered diamonds, which they had been able to smuggle out, if he would help them. He refused payment. Instead, he went back to the ship and explained the situation to the captain, who gave Max permission to provide the refugees with whatever medical assistance he deemed necessary.

Max's ship was scheduled to return to the U.S. after the stopover in Shanghai, so the Penicillin and Sulfa and other drugs would be expendable anyway when they arrived home. So he treated the refugees the best he could and set them up with food and a good supply of medications, which surely helped them survive.

After the war ended, some of those people found Max in New York in order to thank him for saving their lives

Max married Florence (Birdie) Katz (Dave Katz's cousin) during the depths of the Great Depression. They lived in a bedroom in the Katz family's house on 119th Street in Richmond Hill, Queens. The other occupants of the house were Birdie's parents, Birdie's siblings: Oscar, a prominent attorney in local politics, the owner of a large insurance company and owner of multiple taxicab medallions, Frances a divorcee and her little redheaded son George, who was a year or two younger than I was. Also in a tiny separate apartment were Harry (another sibling) and his wife (Essie).

It was a time when families were forced to double up because they could not afford to go it alone.

Oscar was the main financial support of this family. Frances, Birdie, Harry and Essie all worked in his insurance business. Oscar never married, but he did have Aida, a girl friend for many years.

Max had to give up being a pharmacist because he could no longer stand on his feet for the long hours pharmacists do. He had a tendency for blood clots in his legs due to all the cigarette smoking he did when he was in the U.S. Army during World War II.

In the hospital ship's pharmacy where he spent four years, the army supplied him with all the cigarettes he wanted.

All the officers would gather in his pharmacy during down time to smoke and drink the booze that Max concocted from some kind of alcohol with a few drops of iodine for color. Max said, "It tasted and looked like aged Scotch whiskey and wouldn't kill you or make you blind".

By the time Max was discharged from the army, he was smoking four packs of cigarettes a day. It seems the nicotine in the cigarettes had caused the blood clot problem. He went to school, became an insurance broker, and joined the rest of the Katz family in Oscar's insurance business so that he would not have to be on his feet all the time.

The father, we called him Mr. Katz, was a very nice man, I thought. However, when I got a little older and understood what was going on, I heard that he was physically abusing his wife when he got drunk, which was pretty much all the time. Oscar, who was considered the head of the family, had him committed to an institution and that was the last I heard of him. Francis' redheaded son George became a lawyer and the last I heard he was living in New Jersey. After Max died, I lost contact with the Katz family.

Both our cemetery plots are in Mt. Ararat in Farmingdale. When I visit our plot, I go the Katz plot and know who is living or dead by the names on the footstones. Last time I was there, it looked like they had all died, except for George, who, if dead, is in New Jersey.

I loved Max and Birdie. I was the little sister, about eighteen years younger than Max. Several times a year, they would take me out to interesting places and restaurants. They had a very close friend, a retired Russian ballet dancer, who owned a Russian restaurant in Manhattan. What was fascinating about him was that he had no thumbs on his hands. For our entertainment, he would present a short ballet, which he and a tiny ballerina would perform. I was enthralled by these people and of course everything we saw and did that day was memorable. We had Beluga caviar and blini and other typical Russian special foods.

They took me to other interesting places such as the Astor Bar where I had my first Shirley Temple drink while they drank the real stuff. They took me to my first Swedish Smorgasbord Restaurant. And, of course, Radio City Music Hall to see The Rockettes.

Unfortunately, they never had any children. It was too bad because they would have made wonderful parents.

11

SAMUEL #3 SON

Samuel Isaac was the third son born to my parents. I am not sure what year he was born, but I think it was about 1910. My mother (Tzipra) delighted in him because she had an easy delivery with him and he was beautiful from the moment he was born.

Tzipra sewed all the children's clothes by hand until she eventually got a Singer sewing machine with a foot treadle.

Sam was extremely bright and adorable. He learned a lot from Harry and Max, his two older brothers. Harry, the oldest, was very caring and protective of his younger siblings, and they learned from him to be caring and protective of each other.

When Sam was four years old, Tzipra took him to school to register him for kindergarten. He was wearing a sailor suit that she had hand-made for him. She was told that he was too young, that he would have to wait until he was five to enter kindergarten. Tzipra insisted that he was smart enough to go to school now. The clerk called the principal to resolve the problem. When the principal saw him and spoke to him, she saw that he was so smart and so cute in his sailor suit that she decided that he would be a good candidate for kindergarten, thus he entered school at the age of four.

Like Harry and Max, Sam was an excellent student. He was skipped many times and graduated from high school at the age of fourteen. He wanted to pursue a career in medicine to follow in the footsteps of Brother Harry, but, unfortunately, the Great Depression hit around that time and he had to pursue a career that would require less time and money to prepare him to make a living to help support the family. He decided to study accounting at NYU because that was the shortest way to make a living.

When he graduated, the country was in the depths of the Great Depression. In order to qualify for the CPA exam, he was required to work for a CPA for a year. Money was tight and CPAs could not afford to pay someone like Sam, who was learning from them.

Tzipra found a CPA who would let him work the required time for him, but since he couldn't afford to pay, Tzipra agreed to pay the CPA $5 a week to let Sam work for him.

Sam passed the CPA exam with flying colors. His first client was Cousin Harry Meltzer who had a photography business. He couldn't afford to pay Sam, so he paid him with photographs of the family. I have a collection of beautiful sepia tone pictures as a result.

One of the great excitements in our lives was when Sam acquired Major Bowes of the famous Major Bowes Amateur Hour radio program as a client. We were invited many times to the studio to be spectators while the radio program was being broadcast. This was all new at the time and we were thrilled to be there.

Sam had great friends, most of whom were accountants or lawyers. I remember most of them because they would come to our house and Tzipra would make a wonderful meal for them. I remember Dave (darkly handsome) and Hawk (who had a hooked nose), Bob, and two Jacks. One was Jack Passoff and one was Jack Scheinhaus, whom Mom referred to as Jack der Sheiner because his name meant beautiful house, but also because he was good looking, and she could differentiate between the two Jacks this way. This was done privately at home, not when the guys were in the house with us.

I remember one of his friends, Harry Rosenzweig, had a little sister, Anna, the same age as I was. She was a "mongoloid" which, in those days referred to what we call today, Downs Syndrome. I was about five or six when I first met her.

Sam and Harry wanted me to play with her. I did play with her after school for a long time, but I got busy with school and could not spend much time with her after a while. Their mother had died giving birth to Anna, so her care fell to Jack and three older sisters. The sisters never married and Jack married very late in life. I believe they were afraid that Downs Syndrome was genetic and they were afraid to have children.

The five bachelor friends did everything together. They all spent summer weekends at Manhattan Beach in Sheepshead Bay and Sam signed me up as well so I saw them playing handball and tennis and swimming.

Sam was an excellent athlete. He was also a graceful ballroom dancer who knew how to lead his partner. He taught me how to dance.

All my teen-age friends had crushes on Sam and his friends. Sam had a beautiful speaking voice, velvety sounding on the telephone. My friends used to call me on the phone, hoping that Sam would answer so they could hear his voice. Today, Sam's son, Jeffrey has the same voice. I love to speak to Jeffrey on the phone because I feel like I am speaking to Sam.

When the Brooklyn Jewish Center opened on Eastern Parkway in Brooklyn, Sam and his friends joined for the activities, which included a sports center with swimming pool, basketball and handball courts and Saturday night dances for meeting girls.

Jammy Moscowitz was the famous basketball coach who led the team to many victories. Jammy was the older brother of Florence's friend, Rose.

I was about fifteen when Sam signed me up as a member of the Brooklyn Jewish Center. I loved going there to use the sports facilities, particularly the indoor swimming pool. The pool was available to women only on certain days. One of the many rules was that you could not wear a swim suit, but you had to wear a cap to keep your hair out of the water because hair clogs the drains. It was the first time that I swam in the nude, but in spite of modesty, I got used to it. Rules are rules and must be followed if you want to use the facility. Hattie joined as well. The one outstanding memory I have is that I found out that my red-headed sister-in-law, Hattie was really a redhead.

By this time, Sam and his friends, a bunch of eligible bachelors, were in their thirties. Sam was living at home with our mom and me a (teenager) because he, Harry, and Max were supporting us. Harry, Max and Sam were wonderful, responsible sons. They supported our mom until the day she died. Tzipra had no means of income because social security was not in existence when her husband Joe was working. When he became ill and died, Tzipra had to either go on "relief" (now known as welfare) or depend on her grown educated sons to support her and the three younger children. I remember hearing the daughters-in-law grumbling about the fact that their husbands had to chip in to support their mother. It was humiliating for my mother, but she could not help herself. The only one who did not grumble about this was Max's wife, Birdie. Grumble or not, my brothers were true to their responsibility of supporting their mother.

When Sam was about 36, I remember hearing my mom saying to him, "It's time you got married. Don't worry about me. I do not want you to become one of one of those 'fashtunkene alte buchirim' (smelly old bachelors). "

Like magic, shortly after that, Sam brought a lovely woman to meet our mom. This is how it all happened.

That summer of 1946, Sam and his friends joined Wingdale Country Club in upstate New York where they spent their weekends. One weekend, Sam invited my friend, Gilda, there and me for the weekend. He wanted me to meet Ruth, a woman he was interested in to tell him what I thought of her. He valued my opinion, knowing that I liked everybody and would give a good report.

It was Memorial Day weekend, which happened to be Ruth's birthday, so he asked me to find a gift for him to give her. He suggested earrings, which I thought was a good idea. He told me not to spend too much. I worked in the Empire State Building at the time and there were lovely costume jewelry shops on 34th Street. So I spent my lunch hours checking out earrings for Sam's girlfriend. I finally found an elegant pair of marcasite earrings that I thought were appropriate for the occasion. I bought a blue ombre silk scarf in McCreery's as my gift for her because Sam thought she had blue eyes.

Sam's friend Jack Passoff, volunteered to drive me and my friend to Wingdale in his convertible. Gilda and I were excited at first to be in a convertible, but soon found the awful truth that the wind makes a mess of your hair and you cannot have intelligent conversation because of the wind blowing in your mouth. We were happy when the ride was over.

At Wingdale Country Club, a whole group of single females shared a bungalow, including Ruth, her friend, and Gilda and me.

I liked Ruth from the minute I met her. She was kind, considerate, and intelligent and smiled a lot. Sam was impressed with the fact that Ruth had her own toy business. This turned out to be nothing much because she was partners with Aaron, her brother, and it dissolved in a short time.

She liked the earrings I had selected for Sam to give her but I think she was disappointed when Sam handed her the gift, because she thought the box held an engagement ring. Needless to say, when the weekend was over, I had a great report for Sam.

Soon, Sam brought Ruth to meet our mom, who liked her and they were married at Delmonico's the following June 1947. Ruth honored me by asking me to be her maid of honor. Her sister Claire, who was younger than Ruth and already married, was her matron of honor.

12

FLORENCE

Tzipra's fourth child, after three boys, Florence, the girl Mom wanted so much was born in May 1914. She was named for my mother's mother (Feigele). Florence had lemon-yellow hair and hazel green eyes and was the apple of Mom and Pop's eye. She was an excellent student at Thomas Jefferson High School in Brooklyn. She was an excellent swimmer and graceful ballroom dancer.

Unfortunately, she graduated during the depths of the Great Depression.

Instead of going to college, she went to beauty culture school so she could get a job and earn money quickly. She would practice her manicuring and hair cutting skills on the family. We would all, good-naturedly, let her practice cutting our cuticles, and some of us would wind up a bloody mess. It was almost funny to see all of us with band-aids wrapped around our fingers when she got through.

Some of my fondest childhood memories are the Sunday afternoon concerts at the Brooklyn Museum with Florence, my big sister. Very often, one of her friends, Anne, Ray or Rose would accompany us. Either before or after the concert, we would explore different sections of the museum, or, weather permitting; we would stroll through the magnificent Brooklyn Botanical Gardens.

Florence was twenty-four when she met George Levine, whom she eventually married in 1940. Their wedding was held at the Little Oriental on Pitkin Avenue in Brooklyn.

I was a teenager and she honored me by asking me to be her maid of honor. The country was still suffering from the Great Depression, and money was scarce. We couldn't afford to buy me a dress, but I remember borrowing a dress for the occasion from a friend. However, shoes were a problem because I wore size 8, which was big for a young girl in those days. I decided to borrow a pair of silver sandals from Florence, who wore size 7.

We thought I could manage them for one night. That was a mistake! After a short time, my feet were killing me, and I was in agony. I suffered through the evening, but vowed to never wear uncomfortable shoes again.

George came from a distinguished and famous family. His uncle (his father's brother), Dr Samuel A. Levine, was chief cardiologist at Peter Bent Brigham Hospital, also known as Massachusetts General Hospital. His portrait still hangs in the lobby there. He was a Clinical Professor of Medicine at Harvard Medical School and had a fellowship at Rockefeller Institute. He was called in as a consultant for President Franklin D. Roosevelt when he had his heart trouble.

His father's sister, Mildred, was married to Arthur J. Goldberg, Dean of Harvard Law School and presiding judge of the First Circuit Court of Appeals. At one time, he had been nominated for the U.S, Supreme Court.

George's brother, Artie Dunne (stage name) was part of a famous trio, 'The Three Suns". The trio was composed of Artie and two brothers who were his cousins.

Artie played the organ and sang with a lovely Bing Crosby type of voice. One of the brothers played the electric guitar and the other played the accordion. Artie wrote the music for the lyrics of "Twilight Time", which became quite famous and is still played today. The Three Suns traveled all over the world playing their music and were especially famous in Japan.

George was not as accomplished as his famous relatives were. He was introverted and had trouble expressing himself verbally. My amateur psychology diagnosis attributed this to the fact that his mother died giving birth to him and his twin sister Betty. He was brought up by his father, his older sister Selma and grandmother. He probably did not get the attention that a mother would have given him.

George had some hidden talents. He was a wonderful ballroom dancer and missed his vocation by not going professional. As a matter of fact, Florence and George met at Roseland, a famous venue for ballroom dancing. They were beautiful doing the waltz, cha-cha, tango, fox trot. He also wrote poetry and parodies of famous lyrics. He always worked hard, never missed a day's pay and took care of his family.

13

BARNETT (BARNEY)

Barney was the fifth child, born in 1917 after Florence. He was a beautiful child with thick dark hair and a widow's peak.

The house the family lived in was opposite P.S. 84, an elementary school. The street was closed to through traffic because it was considered a school street. A car being driven illegally drove on to this school street. At the age of five, this car, right in front of my mother's eyes, hit Barney, because she happened to be looking out the window at the time. It must have been traumatic for her! He suffered a broken leg, which was put in a cast. When it was all healed after six weeks, he walked with a limp because one leg was shorter than the other.

As far as accident insurance goes, I don't think Barney ever got anything. Today, this would be a million dollar case.

When Mom took him back to the doctor who had treated him, he told her to take him to a specialist. The recommended specialist said that the only way to correct the limp was to break the bone and reset it, so that it would heal properly. Mom didn't like that doctor because he was German and had a very cold, stern way about him. She searched for another specialist and another until she found the one who gave her the answer she could accept.

He said, "Get the child a tricycle and let him ride it a lot. Since he is so young, the exercise will help this leg even out with the other one". And that is exactly what happened. The limp disappeared. As a result of the injury, he was pampered by the family.

Another problem that Barney had was with one eye, which shifted to the side. It is the kind of thing that an ophthalmologist today could probably correct very easily, but he grew up with one eye out of place. My mom claimed that a BB from a BB gun had hit him in the eye, but I don't think that ever happened. She didn't want any of her children to have an imperfection caused by birth.

I do not remember Barney's Bar Mitzvah at the age of thirteen, because I was too young, but I did hear about it later. Bar Mitzvahs in those days were not the elaborate affairs they make today. The custom in those times was for the parents of the Bar Mitzvah boy to bring to "shul" (temple) on that particular Saturday morning, the Oneg Shabbat (refreshments for the congregation) which were usually some pickled herring, schnapps, challah and sponge cake. And that was it! No fountain pens! No expensive gifts!

Unfortunately, Barney grew up during the depths of the Great Depression, when jobs and money were very scarce. He heard about linotype school, where he would learn how to set type for newspapers and magazines. Harry, Max and Sam chipped in to pay the tuition and Barney seemed very adept at it. When he graduated, he learned that he had to join a union, but he could not get into one because it was a father-son arrangement. Your father had to be a union member in order for you to be allowed to join. Unless you belonged to the union, you could not get a job in this field.

He was screwed! I do not know how you learn about something like that before you undertake training and paying tuition. He should have researched it.

He worked for Hattie's father in his dress factory for a while. It was a low-level job and wasn't going anywhere, so he quit.

The next summer, he sold ice cream from a Bungalow Bar truck. That is how he met Edythe, whom he married eventually.

I remember when he asked me go to Steeplechase to meet Edythe.

He knew that I would give a good report about her, so he wanted me to be the first to meet her. When I met Edythe, I liked her immediately. She was pretty, pleasant, smiled and giggled a lot. She had a nice job at the Brooklyn Public Library on Grand Army Plaza in Brooklyn. Barney treated us to all the rides in Steeplechase and lunch. It was a fun day.

When Barney told Mom that he was considering marrying Edythe, Mom's response was "How can you think about getting married? You don't even have a job."

They did get married on December 7, 1940. The Japanese attack on Pearl Harbor, which started World War II, was exactly one year later in 1941.

Sam was working for the War Department in Detroit as a civilian during the war. He told Barney that there was a great need for people in Detroit, Michigan. He suggested that Barney and Edythe come out to Detroit and get the good-paying jobs that were available. They went to Detroit and finally had the opportunity to make some good money. They probably could have saved some of the money they made, but I don't think they did. I don't know what happened after that, but they came back to Brooklyn after the war.

When they were living on Linden Boulevard, I remember babysitting with Fred and Ellen. Fred was a handsome little boy and Ellen was just gorgeous with her blue eyes and blonde hair. I don't remember much about Annie because they moved to Las Vegas when she was an infant.

Cousin Abe Samuels got him a job in Springfield, Massachusetts, where he managed a business and seemed to do well. However he was dissatisfied with something and quit. After several business failures: a luncheonette in Brooklyn, a luncheonette in Manhattan, which were funded by his brothers, he thought he finally found the route to success.

After working for someone else in a dry cleaning store, he thought he could do well with his own store. After a few years in the dry cleaning store, it looked like this was the right thing for him. However, disaster struck! He finally had to leave town because his employees in the dry cleaning store were stealing some of the expensive clothes brought in for dry cleaning. It seems that they would put the stolen clothes on under what they were wearing so the clothes could not be seen. The expression Edythe used was, "They came in skinny in the morning and left fat after work." The customers sued Barney for the loss of the expensive clothing. He closed the store and left town for Las Vegas, hoping that he would not be found. I heard that he was found by collectors, but he had nothing so they could not make him pay. He drove a taxi in Las Vegas for a while. He finally succeeded as a coin laundry entrepreneur in Las Vegas.

Barney was a great teller of stories, which always had a funny ending and had his listeners laughing. He was a great cook and probably should have pursued that field, but it was not as popular then as it is now.

He was a heavy smoker and was exposed to the fumes in the dry cleaning establishment, a deadly combination for illness and death.

14

RHODA (REBECCA, RIFKELE)

Baby Rhoda with Beauty, the Collie

This is the story my mother told me, in a very loving way, of course.

In 1925, when she was 38 years old, Tzipra suspected she was pregnant. When she went to see Dr. Krieger, his first suspicion was that she might have a tumor. When he did determine that she was pregnant, Mom was very upset and embarrassed because she had a son who was already a doctor. She asked Dr. Krieger if there was something he could do to "help" her. His response was "You have five children, so you'll have six"

Tzipra went home and pushed the piano across the living room floor, hoping to abort. But, as she put it, "You stuck like glue. You wanted to come into this world."

She hid the pregnancy as best as she could by covering herself with a large fringed piano shawl, which happened to be the fashion at the time.

She did not tell anybody except her husband, her sister Bella and her sister-in-law, Chevit (Shmiel's wife).

She had decided to be modern by going to the hospital to give birth this time. All the other children had been delivered by a midwife at home.

However, at the last minute, she changed her mind in the belief that prevailed at that time that you would die in a hospital. When labor started, my father got Dr. Krieger to come to the house. After a very difficult labor, my shoulder had been caught and the doctor had to turn me, I was born at 3 A.M. on June 22, 1926. I was born in a caul, which is a membrane covering the fetus and is supposed to bring good luck. History has it that Moses was born in a caul. My mother saved the caul for many years, but eventually it disappeared.

My father was thrilled with the little girl who was named Rebecca for his mother who had died the previous year. The next morning, he went to all the neighbors handing out cigars and telling them, "Se kimt mir a mazel tov!" which means, "Congratulate me!" Since the neighbors did not know that his wife was pregnant, they asked, "Did your dog, Peanuts, have puppies?" It seems that everybody had been able to see Peanuts' pregnancy, but my mother hid hers so well that they were all surprised to hear about it. They couldn't believe it and came in to see if there was really a new baby girl.

Poor Peanuts died giving birth to her puppies the night my mother was giving birth to me. This was Peanuts' fourth pregnancy, and ordinarily my mom would have helped Peanuts with the delivery, but she was busy with her own.

Pop dreaded telling Mom that Peanuts died because Mom was a dog-lover and was very devoted to Peanuts. Mom cried when she heard about Peanuts. However, in her sweet way, she rationalized that she, herself, had been having a terrible time giving birth and thought she would die. She thought she felt the "Malchamuvis"

(Angel of Death) hovering over her while she was suffering. Now she realized that he had come for her and her baby, but took Peanuts and her puppies instead. After I heard that story, I always felt that I owed my life to Peanuts.

Harry thought the name "Rebecca" was too old-fashioned for the times. He suggested that the baby be called a more modern name: Rhoda, which has been my name these many years. Rhoda means "rose" in Greek. Rhododendron is a rose tree.

When I was 16, I had to get a copy of my birth certificate in order to get a job in a defense plant during WWII. That was when I discovered for the first time, that my name was registered as "Rebecca"

All five children were thrilled with this new baby, who was born almost ten years after the fifth child. Harry, who was twenty-one years old and already a doctor at Beth-El hospital, was the most thrilled of all. I looked just like him! When he wheeled me in my carriage, everybody thought I was his child and that my mother was covering up for him by saying I was her child. He got a big kick out of that and delighted in telling me the story.

My mother was very interested in my schooling, just as she was in all the other children's. She always went to Open School Night to meet the teachers and, as she put it "to hear how smart you are". She joined the PTA and was the oldest parent there. The parents of my friends and classmates were ten to twenty years younger. She took me with her to the meetings and I noticed that the Principal, Miss White, and the two assistant principals, Miss Cosgrove and Miss Pidian, treated my mother with great respect.

KINDERGARTEN AND FIRST GRADE IN 1932

I don't remember much about the daily activities in kindergarten in P.S. 219, (K through 6 school), but what I do remember, and it stuck with me, is when my oldest brother Harry asked me about my first day at school, I told him that my teacher's name was Miss Eiermann, he said to me, "her name means "Eggman". That was the first time that I realized that names had a meaning, and that has remained of great interest to me to this day.

My first grade teacher's name was Miss Monahan. She was a beautiful young woman. I don't know if her name had any meaning, I now know that she was probably of Irish origin.

The principal was a very tall, skinny, and severe-looking woman. She was called Miss White. When she appeared, everybody practically stood at attention. She had two assistant principals, Miss Pidian and Miss Cosgrove.

Two assistant principals were probably needed because we had very large classes. We had 48 seats (bolted to the floor with desk in front) in each classroom (6 rows across and 8 rows going back). Usually all were taken.

You will notice that they were all "Miss". Female teachers were not allowed to be married. It is possible that they were secretly married, but showing a pregnancy bump was just not done. Discrimination against married teachers was finally ended with the Civil Rights Act of 1964.

Banks, utilities, telephone companies did not hire married women. If they got married after being hired, they had to leave.

World War II changed a lot of things for women. They took over the men's jobs when the men went off to war. Women drove trucks, trolley cars, worked in factories, did everything that the men had done.

Things certainly have changed for women. Some women now continue their jobs all during pregnancy and practically give birth in the workplace.

15

CATERING LOVINGLY TO A LARGE FAMILY

Nothing was too much trouble for my mother to do for her children if it made them happy. She catered to her large family in every way she could.

Cooking and preparing food for the family was a very important way for mom to show her love.

My brother, Barney, the fifth child, was so skinny, as a child, that he looked like a war orphan. This is hard to believe because he became obese in later life. Mom was worried about him because he was not a good eater.

He would say "No" to everything she offered to make for him. The only food he seemed to like were boneless veal cutlets breaded with egg and matzo meal and fried in oil with fried potatoes.

If he wouldn't eat what she had prepared for the rest of the family, she would ask him if he wanted "veal cucklets" as she called them. After all her work for the rest of the family, she would make the cutlets especially for him and she would "kvell" (look on with pleasure) as he ate with an appetite.

My brother, Maxie, loved boiled beef flanken with "bebelach" (lima beans), barley and dried European mushrooms in soup. Mom made that for him even after he was married and would come for a visit. Nothing pleased him more than to visit and find that Mom had made his favorite dish.

Mom even catered to me, the sixth child. We had no lunch program in elementary and junior high, so I had to come home for lunch. Almost every day, when I came home for lunch, Mom would have ready on the table, two broiled baby lamb chops and a large salad dressed with olive oil and kosher salt because she knew I liked that. Her greatest pleasure was to see me reading a book while I ate.

Sunday mornings were always special in our house. Pop and the boys would drive to a Romanian appetizing store on the Lower East Side. They would come home with matjes herring, and an assortment of Romanian cheeses (brinza, kashkeval, orda, kash). These cheeses are similar to Greek and Italian cheeses. Mom would make a few gigantic "mamaligas" (corn meal cakes or polenta) and Pop would cut them with a string, a knife would stick in the warm corn meal.

We sat around a gigantic table in the dining room. Very often, their Romanian "landsleit" (people from the old country) would join us on Sunday. The one I remember best is Mr. Goldstein, who always arrived with a chocolate Hershey bar for me. I always called him "Hershey" and, of course, I looked forward to seeing him.

Very often, Uncle Shmiel and Aunt Bella and their families would join us as well. There would be laughter with everybody talking at once in very loud voices in Romanian or Yiddish or English.

If there were more than fourteen, my brothers would open up bridge tables at the end of the table for the children. Each of us would take a wedge of mamaliga, pour melted butter and an assortment of cheeses on it and eat it with our fingers. It was absolutely delicious with a piece of salty maatjes herring. For dessert, we had Turkish Delight candy (fragrant satiny marmalade with powdered sugar coating) or home-made coffee cake.

Pop always served his homemade wine and Mom served regular coffee or Kaffee Hag (decaffeinated coffee) in her very large enamel percolators. Nobody drank water, because we had Flatbush water from artesian wells, which was cloudy when it came out of the tap. The cloud, of course, was created by the valuable minerals, which are filtered out of water today. We take supplements to get the minerals that occurred naturally in Flatbush water. The cloud would disappear if you let the water stand a while.

My father used to say, with a twinkle in his eye, "Water is for washing your hands and feet." Instead we had Dr. Brown's Celery Tonic, or Hoffman's cream soda and siphon-bottled seltzer on the table. Sundays were always fun!

16

SHOPPING ON BELMONT AVENUE IN THE 1920'S AND 30'S

Food in my parents' time in Romania was plentiful and good. The food they ate was similar to that of Greece, a neighboring country. When they came to America, they ate pretty much the same kind of foods they had eaten in Romania.

Of course, my mother kept a kosher house. My father was an expert in grilling Romanian tenderloin (skirt) steaks on an open fire in the bottom of the gas range. Fresh fish and chicken and lots and lots of fresh vegetables were on the daily menu. I remember my mom always serving a gigantic salad at dinner every night, dressed with olive oil and kosher salt.

Pop would sear eggplants and peppers on an open gas range flame for "potlejella" (eggplant salad). He made sour pickles, sour green tomatoes, hot red peppers, sauerkraut, and stored them in crocks on a cool windowsill.

When my mother cooked, she prepared enough for a small army. She had six children: four hungry sons, two daughters and Pop. And, of course, everything was made from scratch. There were no prepared foods in those days. She had the most gigantic pots I have ever seen outside of a restaurant.

Her wooden chopping bowl was big enough to hold a 12 pound baby.

Her ladle (which she called a "leffel" or spoon} was big enough to almost fill a large bowl of soup. One of the family's funny stories was that when somebody would say that they were too full for soup, my mother would say, "Ich vel geben dir ein lefel", which meant "I will give you only one spoonful." Of course, my mom meant one ladleful and that person would get a lot of soup.

Mom shopped in neighborhood stores only when she had to, because local stores were too expensive. Money was scarce during the depression years, and Mom saved a few dollars shopping on Belmont Ave. where pushcart peddlers sold everything at lower prices.

Getting to Belmont Avenue in Brownsville was not easy. We did not have a car available. Besides, most women did not drive in the 1930's. I made the trek to Belmont Avenue with my mother many times. We had to walk two long blocks to board the Remsen Avenue bus (the fare was a nickel), which took us to Eastern Parkway, where we transferred to the Pitkin Avenue bus to Watkins Street, and then walked two more long blocks to Belmont Avenue where the streets were lined with pushcarts loaded with all kinds of fresh foods.

Each push cart had a hanging scale, some with a face indicating the weight while some used lead weights in different amounts.

Mom had these two gigantic shopping bags made of some very heavy sturdy material, for carrying her purchases. Before she bought fish from the fish monger, she checked it carefully by smelling it and making sure the eyes were clear. She always bought the whole fish (skin, bones, head and all) but entrails removed. When she bought carp, she made sure it had roe (eggs) so she could make "ikra" (pink caviar), a delicacy, which she dressed with freshly squeezed lemon, olive oil and minced onion. In Greece, this is called "taramasalata". My father's job was to separate the tiny eggs from the placenta, a painstaking job, which he did well and gladly.

In the kosher poultry market, the freshly slaughtered chickens, heads, feathers and all were thrown on large tables. Mom squeezed the chickens to see if they had a lot of fat near the "tuches"(tail). She needed the fat to make "schmaltz" (rendered chicken fat) which made anything delicious when fried in it. Schmaltz was delicious spread on bread or matzo. In the chicken fat rendering process, there were bits of chicken skin and onions, which were called "grievenes" and were a treat to eat.

If Mom felt she could afford it, she would ask the chicken flicker to remove the feathers and singe the pin feathers on the wings and tail so they could be removed easily with an eyebrow tweezer when we got home. The chicken flicker was usually a very poor old woman covered with lice from the chickens she handled all day. She was paid in tips and would get 5 or 6 cents for flicking (removing the feathers from) a chicken.

For meat, Mom went into a kosher butcher shop. We knew it was a kosher shop because it had the Hechsher (Star of David) in the window, which meant it had been checked for Kashruth by a Moishgiech (an official who approved the method of slaughter and cleanliness while reciting certain prayers). She would pick and choose flanken, brisket, veal or lamb.

She had her own manual meat grinder and would buy neck and tenderloin for chopped meat. She did not trust the butcher to grind the meat she had actually purchased, so she ground it herself at home.

Each pushcart specialized in one fruit or vegetable: there was a banana pushcart, one for oranges and grapefruits, one for apples, another for potatoes or certain vegetables, etc. Mom would stuff all her purchases into the shopping bags until they were practically overflowing and very heavy. I don't know how she had the strength to carry them. Very often, she went by herself and I would see her walking home from the corner weighed down by these two heavy bags. I would run to help her. If I went with her, I would help her with the bags by holding one handle while she held the other.

After she finished her shopping, she had to repeat the trip home, taking two buses and walking home. I don't know how she had the energy to do all this. She must have been a very powerful woman. I do not think I could ever do what she did.

17

STORING AND PREPARING FOOD IN THE 1920'S AND 30'S

When Mom arrived home after shopping, she had to find room to store everything and start preparations. Storage was not easy.

Refrigerators did not yet exist. Instead, we had an ice box with a section in it for a large chunk of ice, which was delivered by Tony the Iceman, in a horse-drawn wagon. He would ask Mom in his broken Italian immigrant English, "How much you want today?" Mom would tell him 10 or 15 cents worth. He would use his ice pick to carve the right size from the gigantic chunk of ice on his wagon. He would pick up my mom's order with ice tongs, sling it over his back, which was covered with burlap, and place it in the ice compartment in the ice box. Sometimes, a small piece of ice remained from the last delivery. Thrifty housewife that Mom was, she made sure to add it to the fresh ice. A pan under the ice box collected the drip from the melting ice. This had to be emptied often, and even more often in the summer.

In winter, we took advantage of a cold windowsill, even had a shelf extension added on to the outside of the kitchen window to keep certain foods cool. Eventually, we graduated to a gas powered Kelvinator refrigerator, which had a tiny compartment for ice cubes—no freezer in those days.

Next came preparing the food she had carried home. Mom made her own "gefilte fish". It did not come in jars or frozen blocks. She would buy fresh whole whitefish, pike, carp and a fish she called "buffle". When I asked her what buffle was, she said, "It's called "buffle". I still don't know what it is.

She would take the meat off the bones, save the bones and skin. Then she would chop the fish by hand, adding all kinds of flavorings in one of her gigantic wooden bowls. She had a special enormous pot with a perforated insert under which she would put the fish heads, and bones, which would add flavor to the gefilte fish. Then she would shape the chopped fish into ovals and stuff them into pieces of the skin she had saved. Gefilte means "stuffed", thus stuffed or gefilte fish

Today, they still call it gefilte fish even though it's not stuffed into anything. Then she would cook the fish, safe from the bones, which were under the perforated insert, but still could impart their good flavor into the sauce to help create fish "yoach" (gelled sauce when chilled).

For fried flounder, Mom would buy two very large whole flounders, have the fish monger clean and scale them, then slice each one through the skin and bones into five or six pieces. She would bread each piece with egg and matzo meal and fry it in Crisco or vegetable oil. Delicious! It could be eaten hot or cold. Mom taught me the anatomy of a flounder's skeleton when I was four years old so that I could locate the meat and not choke on the bones. We knew nothing of fish filets in those days. To this day, I prefer whole fish because they are naturally tastier and juicier.

The chicken and meat had to be "koshered", which meant that it had to be soaked, salted, and placed on a drain board before it could be cooked. If it was going to be broiled on an open flame, it did not have to be koshered.

For dinner on Friday, the "forshpeis: (appetizer) was usually home-made gefilte fish and/or "ikra" (pink caviar) (Greek taramasalata), and/or chopped chicken livers served with freshly grated "reitach" (pungently sharp black horse radish), which, when eaten, opened up your sinuses, melted the wax in your ears and popped the lint out of your belly button. My father usually grated the reattach and his eyes would tear from the pungency. The freshly made salad dressed with olive oil and kosher salt was already on the table.

The main course was roast chicken or meat, and of course, chicken soup with "lukshen" (egg noodles) that my mother made herself. She rolled out the noodle dough and Pop would cut it into very thin lukshen. Pop was considered the expert in cutting lukshen very thin. Sometimes he would cut the noodle dough into tiny squares to make "farfel".

My mother always served the soup after the main course. She said she didn't want you to get filled up with soup. If you still had room after the main course, you could wash it down with soup. There were lots of vegetables and potatoes.

For dessert, homemade apple sauce or stewed dried fruit or maybe a sponge or honey cake. Everything was home-made.

The same preparation took place for holidays. For Purim, Mom made hundreds of prune/walnut haman-taschen (triangular stuffed cookies shaped like Haman (a villain)'s hat. Other big holidays were Rosh Hashonah (Jewish New Year) and Yom Kippur (Day of Atonement (fasting and then eating). In addition, of course, Pesach (Passover). I remember carrying the kosher for

Passover dishes, pots and pans up from the basement, where they were stored last year, and bringing down the current "chometzdicke" (not kosher for Passover) dishes, pots and pans to be stored until after Passover.

Reading the HAGGADAH (story of Passover) at the Seder was endless. Pop and the boys read in Hebrew and Pop was a stickler for going through the complete Haggadah. Sometimes, we didn't get to eat until ten o'clock Finally, we opened the door for Eliahu a Novi (Elijah the prophet) to come drink the wine we had prepared for him. Then the children searched for the "afikomen" (surprise dessert) which was hidden.

Very often, Pop's brother and his family or Mom's sister and her family were invited. It was lively and very noisy.

Pop's home-made wine was served at all these dinners. When I was very little, I remember helping with cleanup after the seder was over. If there was a little bit of wine left in any of the glasses, I drank it. I fell asleep on the sofa and didn't get up until late the next day. I had my one and only hangover and have never had more than a couple of sips of any alcoholic beverage to this day.

18

SUMMERS IN THE 1920'S, 30'S AND 40'S

GOING TO THE BEACH

Summers in the 1920's, 30's and 40's could be brutally hot and we had to find ways to keep cool in the city. Air conditioning did not exist yet.

It was still uncomfortably hot in the evening, which made it hard to fall asleep in the bedrooms where the heat had been accumulating all day. The neighbors gathered on the benches in front of our house and chatted until the wee hours of the morning when the temperature would drop a little. I remember falling asleep with my head on the window sill in the front parlor, lulled by the murmuring voices of the neighbors outside my window.

Pop would carry a chair to the corner of our street, hoping to catch a breeze from some direction.

The only cool places were movie theaters where they made one of the first primitive attempts at cooling a large public area. They brought in gigantic cakes of ice (100 lbs.), and delivered them to the basement. A fan would run above the ice and send the cooled air through a vent to the roof where a steam-run fan wheel on the roof delivered cool, fresh air through the heating pipes that were already under the seats.

The sort of air conditioning that we know today was invented by Willis Carrier in 1902. He introduced it in 1925 at the Rivoli Theater in Manhattan.

It took several years for local movie theaters to provide central air conditioning as we know it today. When a theater installed air conditioning, they would hang replicas of icicles from the marquee to advertise that it was COOL in this theater.

If you could afford it, and most people could not, you would send the kids to sleepaway camp. Or, you would find ways to cool off in the city by going to a park or a beach.

During the day, sometimes someone would open a fire pump and water would flood the street. We would cool off in the water.

Some of my friends went to sleepaway camp. My mom would not let me go to one of those. She was afraid that they would not take good care of me or that I would drown. She liked having me with her and I liked it too.

At that time, there was a polio (infantile paralysis) scare in some of the summer camps. This justified my mom's decision to keep me at home.

My friend, Phyllis, contracted polio in summer camp. and as I remember it, one of her legs was much thinner than the other as a result.

Some days, my mom would announce that we were going to the beach. We would put our bathing suits under our clothes and carry a towel.

My mom would prepare the food for the picnic we would have on the beach. Usually, it was just a friend and me. Sometimes, Florence and Barney were available to join us.

We had to take the IRT subway to Franklin Avenue, exit the subway and walk a few blocks to the BMT subway to board the Brighton Beach Line. It took us about an hour to get to the Brighton Beach station, which was elevated. When we descended the steps of the station, there was a large fruit and vegetable market where my mom always stopped in and bought bananas. She loved the over-ripe ones, which were reduced in price. She would also buy really ripe, red tomatoes.

We walked two blocks to the beach and Mom would set a blanket down on the sand in what became our territory. We youngsters would quickly take our clothes off and couldn't wait to jump into the surf. Brighton Beach's waves were not very high, but it was enough for us to safely enjoy jumping and floating and practice swimming.

In those days, it was safe to leave your belongings unguarded on the beach.

However, Mom always kept an eye on our blanket. After a while, we would all come out of the water, hungry for the goodies that Mom had packed that morning. Mom had gone to the bakery before we had even awakened and bought fresh rolls and fresh crumb buns.

She had breaded and sautéed veal cutlets to a golden brown and packed them in several layers of waxed paper. Plastic wrap and containers did not exist yet. She packed sour pickles that Pop had made in a small jar. We all stood and watched her as she took out a knife and cut a roll for each of us and put a veal cutlet in it to create the most delicious sandwich imaginable. We each got a sour pickle and/or a ripe tomato that she had just bought.

Dessert was a ripe banana and/or a crumb bun. I do not remember what we drank, but it was probably soda in a bottle that Mom would send us to buy from one of the concessions on the boardwalk. After a while, some kid would come along selling Eskimo Pie ice cream pops and Mom would buy one for each of us.

We felt nice and cool. The sun felt good on our wet bathing suits. We all got sunburned the first time at the beach, and had to suffer the red sunburn, which blistered and peeled, and then we all turned nice and tan and healthy looking. At that time, we did not know that we were damaging our skin for which we would have to pay the penalty later. I am all freckled on my shoulders and hands due to "adolescent solar indiscretion "as the dermatologist put it. Some people have suffered more serious effects from sun exposure.

We had to wait at least an hour after eating before we could go back in the water. We would spread a towel on the sand and soak up the sun on our wet swim suits. Sometimes we would play ball or build sand castles or play other games that were appropriate on the beach.

When the hour was up, we went back in the water and enjoyed a second round of cool water pleasure. About four or five o'clock, we would get ready to go home. We were all sandy, but we put our clothes on over our damp bathing suits, knowing that we would shower when we got home. We had all enjoyed a lovely cool day, including Mom.

19

SUMMER IN THE 20'S, 30'S AND 40'S

TRIP TO THE MOUNTAINS

Getting to the farm in the Catskill Mountains was quite a production. We could have traveled there on the Erie Lackawanna Railroad or Greyhound bus, but we had too much stuff to take with us for a whole summer.

Sometimes one of my brothers would load our car and drive us there.

If they couldn't do it, my mom engaged a hacker (driver) for the four-hour trip, to drive us there in his old eight-passenger over-sized Packard. Other families would share the car with us. The hacker could pack as many as twelve people into the car: three in front (including him), plus three on the jump seats, and three in the back seats. As many as three kids would sit on their parents' laps in the back seats. I was usually on my mom's lap.

All the suitcases and boxes with pots and pans were loaded on the luggage rack on the car's roof and on a fold-down luggage rack behind the trunk, which was also packed. It was quite a load!

I was a little girl, so did not know the exact route he took to get us there, but I do remember going through the Holland Tunnel, which was scary, because I knew we were under water and I saw water running down the tiles lining the sides of the tunnel. Of course, there was no Thruway or Quickway.

I noticed the mountains ahead and the Erie Lackawanna Railroad on our right. The hacker mentioned that he was heading for Route 17.

The next thing I remember is the hacker announcing that we were approaching the infamous Wurtsboro Hill, which had the reputation as a very steep hill, hard on your car. He put the car in low gear and started the climb. Along the side of the road, we saw several stalled cars with smoke coming out of their engines. But our car kept going. When we got to the top of the hill, he heaved a sigh of relief and so did we. Then I saw signs for Route 17.

Soon afterwards, we would make a pit stop at the Black Apple or the 999 for the rest rooms and refreshments. The Black Apple Inn and the Black Apple Hotel (formerly Brown's Hotel) were owned by Jerry Lewis' family, where he got his start as a "toomler" (a lively performer) entertaining the guests. The 999 was kosher and my mom preferred it, but we went where the hacker took us.

Then we got closer to what was called the Borscht Belt, the Catskills where Jewish families vacationed at hotels and boarding houses. We passed through Fallsburgh and then South Fallsburgh and then the tiny strip shopping area called Woodbourne. We were almost at our destination!

I knew we were on the right track when we were driving on a dirt road, which led to the farm. Finally, another half hour later, we saw a sign on a hill which read "Friedman's Fair View Farm House". We had arrived!

20

SUMMER IN THE 20'S, 30'S AND 40'S

SUMMER ON A FARM

One of the most wonderful experiences of my childhood (age 4 to 10) was spending many summers on a working farm owned by Mr. and Mrs. Friedman. In order to make some extra money, they rented their eight bedrooms to families like mine. They named the farm "Friedman's Fair View Farmhouse". The Friedman family, which consisted of the parents and their five children: (in order, oldest to youngest) Masha, Leia. Goldie, Leibl (the only boy) and Nancy, who slept on mattresses set on the floor of the attic. Leibl was a little older than I was and Nancy was a little younger than I was.

Each bedroom had a wall-hung sink, with a mirror above it, a closet and two beds. There were folded cots in a storage room in case you needed more beds for visitors. There was one large bathroom for everybody in the hall. It had a bathtub with overhead shower, large sink, toilet, and window. Some scheduling was necessary for so many people to use one bathroom. I don't remember any fights, but I did hear complaints. There were also privies (outhouses) available at the back of the house.

We did not have to use the bathtub very often, because almost every day we would go swimming in the Neversink River, four pastures away, which was about a mile away. The river had crystal clear water, so clear that we could see baby fish swimming in it.

The house had a very large community kitchen, which was equipped with a two-burner gas range and a small icebox for each individual family. In a corner of the kitchen was a gigantic wood-burning stove with oven, which everybody could use. The aromas on Fridays were delicious because the women would use the oven to bake challahs, pies, cookies and cakes, roast chicken and meat to have available in case there were visitors for the weekend.

Fresh ice had to be placed in the ice box every few days delivered by Sal the ice man. Mrs. Friedman had a small store where she sold groceries. Every once in a while, Friedman would drive his truck into Woodbourne or South Fallsburgh and take some of the women along so they could shop. None of the guests had cars. Besides, most women did not drive at that time.

In addition to the kitchen, there was a very large community dining room with eight round tables and chairs. Mealtime was a lot of fun.

Everything smelled mouth-watering delicious. The moms always prepared too much, so they would offer food to the other residents. I tasted some wonderful food this way. This was like camp, but your mom was there. I remember Mrs. Heller, a tiny generous woman, who barely spoke English, and who always made too much food for herself and her teen-age daughter, Ruthie, who was Florence's age. She would go around offering her delicious food to everybody. She seemed to get a lot of pleasure doing this.

She was much loved and admired. Everybody was inspired by Mrs. Heller and did the same, but Mrs. Heller's was the best.

Mr. Friedman hung flypaper in the dining room to attract the annoying flies who were always buzzing around where there was food. Fly paper was sticky and when a fly landed on it, it could not extricate itself.

After a few days, the flypaper was covered with stuck flies and Mr. Friedman would put fresh ones up. This helped keep the fly population down without harmful sprays.

Water was supplied to the house by ice melting on the mountains. It was sparkling pure, delicious and ice cold. I don't remember anybody getting sick from the water.

The set-up of individual cooking earned this type of place the moniker "KUCHALAIN" (with a gutteral CH), which, literally translated from Yiddish means "COOK ALONE" or "DO YOUR OWN COOKING".

We called the place "Friedman's Fair View Farmhouse Hotel Kuchalain". Instead of going to an expensive hotel, poor Jewish families could afford a whole summer in the country in this way.

Mr. Friedman had arranged with the Hotel Belvedere up on a hill to permit us to attend the shows at the hotel on Saturday nights. When Saturday night came, we got all dressed up, took our flashlights, and walked the half mile up the hill on the dirt road to the Belvedere.

I marveled at the sky at night. I saw more stars than I had ever seen in Brooklyn and could even recognize the Big and Little Dippers.

There was a live band at the hotel so that everybody could dance.

The hotel benefited from our attendance because we bought soda and snacks from the food concession in the casino. All had a good time!

21

BACK TO NATURE
ON THE FARM

Mrs. Friedman (the farmer's wife) would give us kids bags of chicken feed to feed the chickens who were roaming around. It was an experience to see chickens peck at the chicken feed that we threw on the ground. She would also let us go into the chicken coops with Leibl and Nancy to gather the eggs that the chickens had laid.

Once a week the "shochet" (ritual slaughterer) would slaughter some chickens for Mrs. Friedman to sell to the residents. She made sure that we did not see the 'shochet' cut the jugular vein in the throats of the chickens, which is the accepted method for slaughter of an animal in the Jewish religion. When the mothers bought a chicken, they had to kosher it by soaking and salting it and placing it on a downward slanted draining board before cooking it. There was always delicious chicken soup and, of course, roast or fried chicken

The cows on this farm were dairy cows, and had to be milked by hand. Nothing automatic in those days. These cows had won a blue ribbon at a competition. NYS health inspectors periodically checked out the Friedman dairy farm and gave it high marks.

Mr. Friedman tried to teach us how to milk the cows. Leibl was good at it, but the rest of us were a little scared and repelled. So we did not really learn how to do it.

Shep was the German shepherd-collie mix dog who helped Mr. Friedman or Leibl bring the cows into the barn from the pastures where they had been feeding all day, Around four o'clock, Mr. Friedman would go to the edge of the pastures and shout, "HOOOEEE". Shep would run into the pasture. The cows, their udders heavy with milk, would turn toward the direction of the barn, still grazing. They would obey Shep who was herding them into the barn.

This was milking time and Mr. Friedman and Leibl would wash the cows' udders before milking them. Mr. Friedman always had a glass of frothy warm milk fresh from the cow for us.

There was a pond with ducks and geese. They all had babies at this time and we would watch the baby ducklings and goslings follow their parents in a line.

In August, the huckleberries were ripe for the picking. The women and children would go into the cow pastures where the huckleberry bushes were laden with tiny purple huckleberries, which were smaller than blueberries.

We children had small pails to fill and the moms had glass jars to fill with the berries. We would eat a few while we were picking. When the jars and pails were pretty full, we would go back to the kitchen, where the moms would decide whether to make huckleberry pie or jelly, or just to sugar some for the kids with some sour cream topping. My mom soaked some berries in some kind of alcohol to create brandy, which was good to kill the pain of a toothache, when soaked with a piece of absorbent cotton and placed on the tooth.

Also in August, the many apple orchards were laden with all kinds of red apples. We would follow Leibl, climbing trees and picking up red apples that had fallen off the trees. We would fill paper bags, and, of course, eat a few. We would bring the apples back to our moms, who would make apple sauce or pie. My mom made an especially delicious apple cake. Yum!

22

INNOCENT CREATIVE ACTIVITIES ON THE FARM

There were always many children, including the farmer's five, to play with. We had to use our own imagination since there were no arts and crafts counselors. We couldn't buy any equipment because there were no shops to buy any equipment from. We had to use what was available. We taught each other what we knew and looked to Leibl when he was not working on the farm, to do interesting things that he knew. We would wander the fields and pastures. We picked wildflowers and brought them home for our moms to put in a bottle on the table.

I knew how to make a necklace out of dried cantaloupe and honeydew seeds, which we would then paint with nail polish. I taught all the kids how to do it. Soon, everybody was wearing one of these necklaces.

We would look for small red stones that we could rub on large stationery rocks until we could shape it into a heart, diamond, oval or round shape. We would engrave a message on the stone with a hatpin, and then poke a hole into it with the hatpin to thread a string through, and hang it around our necks. It would take hours, sometimes days to get the red stone into the desired shape. Some of them were really beautiful—works of art. It kept us busy.

Leibl taught us how to make butterscotch. He mixed a cup of sugar and a cupful of butter and cooked it over a slow flame until it was smooth and silky. Then he turned it out into a tin foil container and let it cool. Then we went out to the pipe that carried the mountain water to the farm and let the water run over it to cool it. When it cooled, it was hard in one big chunk of butterscotch. Leibl cracked it into bite size pieces with a rock and gave us each a piece. We were amazed because we never saw anybody make candy before. It was delicious!

Rainy days were the most fun. We sat on the wraparound porch on the triple-layer paint-covered rocking chairs and played all sorts of games. I learned how to play cards on rainy days. We played casino, concentration, rummy, poker, Honeymoon Bridge, old maid. We played "statues" where you whirled someone out and they struck a pose and you had to guess who they were. These were all innocent games that we could learn from.

Almost every day at about three or four o'clock, we would hear the bells of a no-name ice cream truck. We would run to get money to buy a pop or a cup of ice cream. Freezers were not yet readily available. We certainly had no freezer facilities on the farm, so this was our only access to ice cream. Yum!

Occasionally, Harry would pile whoever was home into the Packard after his office hours, and surprise us with an overnight visit. Besides Harry, it was usually, Florence, Barney and Sam if they were not working, and Pop if he was feeling well enough for the trip. They would take a refreshing swim in the Neversink River, have some of Mom's delicious food and just relax. They slept anywhere, very often in the hammocks that were strung between the trees. They had a short respite from the stifling heat of the city, and left the next morning. It was fun to be surprised.

Mom loved her hammock. She would lay in it reading her newspaper which she held with one hand, with her other hand scratching Shep behind the ears as he lay on the ground next to her, resting before bringing the cows in. Mom would give him snacks and pat and scratch him. No wonder he loved her.

One afternoon, somebody had taught us how to make wild flower wreaths to wear in our hair. The wreath was held together by winding the stems, which had a tendency to unwind, and had to be rewound. I went to my mom to ask her to fix my wreath, and I accidentally stepped on Shep's paw. He immediately reacted by biting me on my shin, almost to the bone. We learned later that he had a thorn in that paw. Mom realized that the wound in my leg was beyond her first aid, which was hydrogen peroxide, so she called Harry, who said he would come that evening.

Harry arrived in the middle of the night. He cauterized the three deep holes in my shin. His main concern was that Shep might be infected with rabies, which would give me hydrophobia, unless I got a series of painful shots in my abdomen that Louis Pasteur worked on. The ASPCA took Shep away for rabies testing, which took two weeks at the time.

Mr. Friedman was worried that my mom would sue him and that he would lose his farm. My mom reassured him that she would not sue. It was late in the summer so we packed up and went home. My leg took a long time to heal, because a dog's canine teeth are long, which made the wound very deep. I am a nonagenarian and still carry the scars from the time I was bitten at the age of six. Sadly, when we went back the next summer, Mr. Friedman told my mom that he had to put Shep down because he was afraid he would bite someone else and they might sue. We were heartbroken and cried.

23

THE BUNGALOW ON CONEY ISLAND

One summer in early 1930's, Mom decided that we could keep cool on Coney Island, a summer resort beach about an hour by train from where we lived.

We rented a bungalow on the corner of Beach 27th Street and Surf Avenue, one block from the beach and the cool waters of the Atlantic. The Surf Avenue Trolley passed our corner and took you to the Coney Island Station of the BMT elevated train. It was very convenient for the family to go to work and come home and cool off. Sam, Florence and Barney stayed for the weekend.

What I remember is that there was sand everywhere. Mom had a constant battle sweeping and shaking out everything to get rid of the sand.

Next door were the Hines family. There were mother and father, two really tall, husky sons, (I think they were detectives), and Mary, who was about a year older than I was. We all got very friendly and had a nice summer with these neighbors.

Mary and I spent our days at the beach, swimming and playing in the sand. Mom and Mrs. Hines would offer food to each other. That's when Mrs. Hines learned that we were Jewish because my mom would not accept any ham or meat from her. I suspect that we were the first Jews they befriended, just as they were the first non-Jews we had befriended.

There was a carousel on the boardwalk at Beach 27th Street, and every time my brothers came out, they would put little me on a horse, thinking I liked it. But I really did not and couldn't wait for it to stop so I could get off. I didn't say anything because I sensed they got pleasure seeing me on the horse and I didn't want to spoil it.

One day, after swimming, I sat scratching my head. Mom checked my scalp and guess what? My thick black hair was infested with millions of lice. Mom immediately called my brother Max, the pharmacist, who came out the next day with kerosene, which was the accepted treatment for lice in those days. A lit match would have made my hair catch fire.

Mom washed my hair with the kerosene, and then she had to use a fine comb to comb out the lice and nits (tiny little white lice eggs that clung to the hair). The lice were very hard to kill, and as my mom fine-combed them, she cracked the live ones with her fingernail on the comb. It took a couple of weeks to get rid of the lice completely, and Max came out to check on me periodically.

In spite of the lice and the sand, it was a nice summer. When it was time to say "Goodbye" to the Hines family, Mrs. Hines said she would invite us all for Thanksgiving. We exchanged addresses and telephone numbers and went home.

I was very young and this is how I remember it. Thanksgiving arrived and true to her word, Mrs. Hines invited us for Thanksgiving dinner at their house in Jamaica, Queens. This event must have been before Pop had his stroke. Pop drove Mom and me in the front seat of the model T Ford, and Florence and her friend Rose sat in the rumble seat.

Mrs. Hines had prepared a wonderful dinner and there was a lot of drinking, especially by the Hines men and Rose. For dinner, there was a beautiful roasted ham and a turkey with all the trimmings. Mrs. Hines forgot that Mom was kosher and was disappointed that she would not eat the ham or the turkey. There were plenty of other side dishes that Mom would eat.

It became a pretty drunken party after a while because the Hines men and Rose were really indulging. I renewed acquaintance with Mary. All in all, it was a lovely evening, and soon it was time to go. My family got into the Ford. Rose needed help getting into the rumble seat.

It started to snow before we were half-way home, so Florence and Rose had to cover themselves with the tarp stored in the rumble seat for this reason.

When we arrived home, Rose was in a drunken stupor. I had never seen anything like this before. She needed help getting out of the rumble seat and was cursing and grumbling half awake. When she was out of the rumble seat, she was barefoot in the snow. It was comical seeing her, obviously drunk, standing barefoot in the snow and mumbling, "Where are my shoes?" We concealed our giggles. We had to search for her shoes and found them with some difficulty, because they had slid down to the very front of the rumble seat floor, which is way down in the car under the driver's seat.

Rose slept on the couch at our house because she was too drunk to take the train home. She kept us all awake with her snoring.

To me, this must have been a very memorable event, because almost 90 years later, I remember everything.

My mom reciprocated by inviting the Hines family for Friday night dinner.

We stayed in touch for a while, but as those things usually go, we lost touch after a while.

24

WINTERS IN THE 1920'S AND 30'S ON EAST 92 ST.

Winter activities for us kids in the 1920's and 30's, as I remember, consisted of staying indoors as much as possible to keep warm and reading.

Occasionally, Mom would decide to visit one of her friends a few blocks away. Not everybody had a telephone, so Mom could not call to say we were coming or even if we were welcome. I remember my mom dressing me in a snowsuit, scarf, galoshes and a pupke hat (a hand-knit woolen hat with pupkes [woolen pom-poms] on top). We would walk in the snow to visit Mrs. Gray (changed from Grabolowsky). It was so cold that after walking a few blocks, my feet became numb and I was glad when we arrived.

My mom would ring the bell and when her friend opened the door and saw us, she was happily excited. Within minutes of our arrival, the table was covered with all kinds of food, with Mrs. Gray encouraging us to "Eat! Eat!" They would have their conversation, either in Yiddish or English. I listened very quietly, never interrupted, was a little pitcher with big ears, and was always a welcome guest.

Sometimes my friends and I would go belly-whopping on our sleds down a steep hill created by a builder who had excavated a very deep hole on an empty corner lot in preparation for building the foundation for an apartment house. The apartment house was never built that I remember.

Occasionally, the boys would have snowball fights, with the girls as their targets. Most of us could not afford to buy ice-skates, so ice-skating was out. Skiing did not exist in our area so that was also out.

School buses were provided only for handicapped children. We walked to school in all kinds of weather. In elementary school and Junior High, there was no lunch program. You either brought lunch or walked home for lunch.

When the house was bought in 1926, the main fuel for heating homes was coal. We had a gigantic oven in the basement into which you had to throw shovels full of coal, where it would burn and send heat up into the house through steam radiators. This was called steam heat. As the coal burned, ashes would form and fall to the bottom of the oven, which had to be shoveled out all the time before the ash pile got too high and block the heat.

The coal was delivered by a truck, which had barrels in it for the driver to fill with coal and roll to the house where there was a special window that he could open. Under the window in the basement was a chute. When the coal was sent through the window, it would go onto the chute and into the enclosed coal bin, which could hold a few weeks' supply of coal.

The coal delivery business was big business, just as coal mining was in those days. We had graduated from cold water flats to steam heated apartments.

Here was one of the problems. Somebody had to throw the shovels of coal into the oven. Mom hired LeRoy, a black janitor, whose job was to feed the oven with coal and to remove the ashes from the bottom of the oven, and get the ash-filled barrels up the basement steps for the garbage collections on certain days. He worked for several homes on our block, and lived in the basement of one of the neighbors. He was a bit sullen, but everybody said he was reliable and honest. Who wouldn't be sullen with that kind of job?

Every once in a while, he didn't show up. We learned that he would get drunk and have to sleep it off. If it was really cold weather, the landlord (my mom), by law, would have to provide heat for the tenants, whether the janitor showed up or not. Sometimes, one of my brothers was available to replace LeRoy to shovel coal and remove ashes. If the boys were not available, Mom would shovel the coal herself. I remember seeing my mom, this little woman, lifting the coal-laden shovel with difficulty. I was too little to help her, and would only get in her way. After a while, LeRoy would return.

We were living in the house for about seventeen years when we heard about oil heat.This meant that coal would be eliminated replaced by oil, which would be delivered through a pipe to the basement where an all new mechanism would provide heat for the house. The only problem for my mom was that it cost a lot of money to convert from coal to oil heat.

Pop passed away before she had to make the decision to convert. She sold the house shortly after Pop died and was spared the expense of conversion. She made no profit on the sale because the house was old, somewhat outdated and real estate values in our neighborhood had dropped.

We moved to an apartment at 961 Eastern Parkway on the sixth floor, so Mom had to accept using the elevator. She did it without a problem, considering that a short time ago she would use neither an elevator nor an escalator.

Of course, the apartment was very small for the three of us (Mom, Sam, and me) compared to the house we had come from. The worst part for Mom was the very tiny kitchen, but she cooked up a storm anyhow. The building was one block from the Utica Avenue Station of the IRT, so, for me it was very convenient, because I was working in the Empire State Building by then, and I was happy there.

Things keep changing. Now I have solar panels to provide my electric power and gas delivered automatically for my heat. I may convert my heating system to electric to help the environment and to foil the Oil Cartel.

I am thinking about it. That's progress!

25

BRINGING RELATIVES TO AMERICA

As my father prospered, he planned to bring the rest of his and my mother's family out of Romania to America. He paid for and sent tickets for his brother, Shmiel, and for my mother's sister, Bella, to come to America in 1914. My mother's best childhood friend, Shifra, traveled with them.

Shmiel left his wife, Chevit and their three children in Romania, intending to work here as a carpenter, to earn enough money for their tickets very soon. Unfortunately, the events of World War I prevented their leaving Romania until the war ended in 1918.

Shmiel's son, Harry, told us stories of the hardships they endured during World War I in Romania. Mail was not reliable, so any money

Shmiel sent to support the family did not always get there.

To make some money, Chevit cooked food that Harry, a little boy at the time, would, at great danger to himself, sell to both the Allied and German troops in their trenches.

In 1918, at the end of WWI, my father lent money to Shmiel to buy tickets to send to Romania for his family, which was composed of his wife Chevit and three children: Rose, Harry and Abe, to come to America. The understanding was that Shmiel would work as a carpenter to pay my father back for four tickets. Unfortunately, Shmiel had a reputation of liking his schnapps and being kind of lazy. He never repaid my father, who carried a grudge against him for this all his life. For many years, my father would not speak to Shmiel, until one Yom Kippur, my mother and Chevit forced them to make up. But Shmiel never did repay the loan.

The family in California, that I love dearly, should be aware that you are all here enjoying the beauty and freedom of this country because my father paid for the tickets to bring your family here.

I was a little girl when all this was happening, but I always loved my Uncle Shmiel and first cousins Rose, Harry and Abe.

Cousin Harry (to differentiate him from my brother Harry), was a teenager when he arrived here. He worked hard to make money to educate himself. One job was as a door-to-door brush salesman. He contracted anthrax from contact with the brushes, which were made of animal bristles.

Anthrax can be fatal, but luckily, he recovered. Eventually, he put himself through law school and became a prosperous lawyer, making big deals for large corporations, such as Bulova Watches, which is the only famous one I can recall.

I remember how much I loved visiting Uncle Shmiel and Aunt Chevit in their apartment on Eastern Parkway. Later on, when Cousin Harry prospered, they moved to Riverside Drive. They had an apartment on a high floor. When we visited, I remember my mom running around and closing all the windows, for fear that I would fall out of a window.

I also loved visiting Cousin Rosie, her husband Sam and her family in their apartment on Stone Avenue in Brownsville, where I could see my cousins, Ruthie, Sonny and Tzippie. I admired and was fascinated with Ruthie because she was already a budding artist and I could see her art work.

Harry was very devoted to his mother. When she suffered from severe arthritis and was told to live in a warm climate, Harry moved the whole family to Los Angeles, where, supposedly, his mother felt better.

That is where Shmiel's family is now.

My mother's sister, Bella, was unmarried when she arrived in America. In a short time, my mother became a "shadchen" (matchmaker) and matched her up with Benny Berkowitz, an iron worker who was a landsman (fellow Romanian). They married and eventually had three sons.

Shifra, my mother's childhood friend, also was single, so my mother matched her up with another landsman. They got married and went into the laundry business.

The descendants of Shmiel and Bella are lucky that my father led the way to America, so that their families could grow and prosper.

We do not know what happened to the rest of my parents' families. We suspect that they were victims of the holocaust, because when the Nazis invaded Romania, the resident Romanians welcomed them and helped kill Jews.

The Jewish population of Romania practically disappeared during WWII.

26

BECOMING AMERICAN CITIZENS

In the 1930's I recall that in order to qualify to apply for citizenship, you had to declare your intention to become a citizen and establish residency for a certain period. Then five years later, you had to take a test. Maybe it is different now, but that is how it was then.

My mother and father had already declared their intention to become citizens. After five years, my mother heard that they were giving citizenship preparation classes in my elementary school.

She decided to go to the class and asked me to go with her. My father was reluctant to go because he had had a stroke and his speech was halting, so my mom went alone with me.

We shared a seat in a classroom. My mom caught on very quickly and studied the sheets about American history that were distributed. In a short time, she was ready to take the written test, which would be graded by the instructor. Mom passed easily and a date was set for the swearing-in ceremony at which time, you still had to answer some oral questions from the judge.

The swearing-in ceremony took place in a courthouse someplace in Brooklyn. The whole family (all six of us and Pop) got all dressed up to attend this momentous event.

We were all very proud of my mother when she answered the judge's questions and was handed her citizenship papers.

We went home and toasted the new U.S citizen. My mom made a big family dinner party in honor or the occasion.

A while later, Pop, encouraged by Mom's success, followed in her footsteps. I went with him to the citizen preparation class at my elementary school. He passed the written test very easily. A date was set for the swearing-in ceremony. Again, the whole clan got all dressed up to attend Pop's swearing-in ceremony

When Pop came before the judge, who asked him a simple question, Pop knew the answer, but hesitated because of his halting speech.

When the judge looked at him questioningly, my brother Harry rose and asked permission to speak. The judge asked him, "Who are you?" Harry explained, "Your Honor, I am this man's oldest son. I am a doctor. My father has had a stroke and has difficulty speaking." Pointing to the rest of us, he said, "This is another son, who is a pharmacist and another who is an accountant. And these three children are still in school."

Before Harry could say any more, the judge spoke directly to my father and said, "With such a wonderful family, you have enriched this country and made a fine contribution to the United States of America. You are granted citizenship and will be sworn in," Pop was so happy that he cried. We were all ecstatic and laughed and cried with him for joy.

And so, my parents had accomplished their dream of becoming American citizens. Of course, Mom made another big citizenship celebration dinner for the family and we toasted the new American citizen.

27

SPELLING BEE

I am a nonagenarian and remember the spelling bee conducted by Sam Levenson, who was the teacher in my Spanish class at Samuel J. Tilden High School in Brooklyn in 1940.

This was before he became a famous stand-up comedian. He was a wonderful teacher and kept us amused with stories about his family. When you heard laughter in the school corridors, it was coming from Mr. Levenson's class.

It was the last day of school and Mr. Levenson announced that since we had covered all our required material, we would have a spelling bee. He took a five-dollar bill out of his wallet and held it up for all to see. He said, "Whoever wins the spelling bee will get this $5 bill as a prize."

We were all very excited. He had a list of words prepared. He started with Marvin Adelson who sat first row first seat, because we were seated alphabetically and went all the way to Rita Zimmerman in the sixth row last seat.

The first round of words was pretty easy and only half the class was eliminated. The second round was harder and another half were eliminated. After several rounds, we finally got down to two, of which I was one. Sidney P. was the other.

We had six rounds of difficult words until Sidney misspelled "unbelievably". I had to spell it correctly, which I did. But I had to spell one more word in order to win. The word I was given was one that I had never heard before. If I had been taught about the birth of Jesus and the three Magi bearing gifts, I would have recognized and spelled the next word correctly. But I was a Jewish girl who learned about Moses and Passover and Chanukah. Christmas in my neighborhood was a holiday for trees and music and presents.

The word between me and winning the $5 was "myrrh" (definition: an aromatic resin used to treat wounds and, in a time before deodorants, to make dead bodies smell better). The gifts the Three Magi brought to Baby Jesus were gold, frankincense and myrrh (all very valuable at the time). Never having heard the word before, I, of course, did not spell it correctly and so I did not win the spelling bee.

I think that Mr. Levenson knew his five dollar bill was safe because the kids in this Jewish neighborhood had never heard of frankincense and myrrh.

28

THE RABBI

It was the 1930's, I was about six or seven years old and this is what I remember.

Many European Jews were fleeing the Nazis. Rabbi Israel Twersky, a member of the famous, greatly respected rabbinical Twersky family, was brought to America by the Joint Distribution Committee, one of the Jewish organizations which helped bring Jews out of Europe to the safety of our country.

They bought him a house on Lincoln Place just off Utica Avenue in Brooklyn. It was an all-brick two-story semi-detached house with a large front porch. The main level was set up as a synagogue with a raised bima (a stage) from which the Rabbi conducted the religious services.

Since the Rabbi was orthodox, the women were separated from the men during services. A back room was set up for the women. There was even a back door for the women to enter so that they did not have to walk through the main area filled with men. In the tradition of separating men and women, Jews and Muslims are not very far apart.

The Rabbi had five handsome, religious sons, ranging in age from teenagers to five-year-old Motl, the youngest.

One of the teenagers was blind. The story was that when the family was fleeing the Nazis, the boy contracted scarlet fever, which he survived but left him blind.

The Rabbi had very kind, wise and understanding eyes, and a long red beard mixed with grey. His beard had tobacco stains around his mouth from the cigarettes he smoked constantly. His face was much wrinkled and he was very skinny. He looked like he carried all the cares of the world on his shoulders.

The Rebbitzin (Rabbi's wife) was a beautiful, buxom woman who would join the other women in the back room reserved for women. It was here that she complained about the Rabbi because he gave her sons only, no daughters. She was way ahead of her time because we now know that the male sperm determines the sex of the fetus. This was only one of the many reasons she complained about him, which she enumerated willingly. She complained bitterly that he was a miser, did not give her enough money and that he was a "bazer" (a mean and angry person).

The women continued to chat while the Rabbi conducted services in the main area. The women treated the Rebbitzin with great respect and listened very politely while she went on complaining.

Since I was always with my mother, I overheard all the conversations. They spoke in Yiddish, which I understood. I listened, but I never said anything nor did I repeat anything I heard. Almost 90 years later, I am finally telling the story.

It seems that when the shiddach (match) was made in Europe, the Rebbitzin's family was extremely wealthy but uneducated and considered it a great honor for their daughter to marry a learned, educated rabbi, who was not expected to be rich or to make a lot of money.

He was supposed to be supported by the bride's family while he studied and interpreted the Torah. In Judaism, the Torah is the law of God as revealed to Moses and recorded in the first five books of the Old Testament: Genesis, Exodus, Leviticus, Numbers and Deuteronomy. The word "Torah" means to teach and is the source of the Ten Commandments.

Traditionally, a Torah is meticulously hand-written by a scribe in beautiful Hebrew letters on a parchment scroll, which is wound around two carved wooden poles. The poles are unwound when the Torah is being read every Saturday and on certain holidays. The Torah is a greatly treasured possession in a Jewish temple.

In Europe, the population was mostly illiterate and uneducated. A rabbi was honored and respected as a man of god. The father-in-law of a rabbi had bragging rights. He could proudly refer to "My son-in-law, the Rabbi"

Everything changed for the Rabbi, the Rebbitzin and their family when they had to flee Europe with just their lives. They arrived penniless and had to be supported by the Jewish community. As a result, the Rabbi was very poor and the Rebbitzin complained.

In those days, a synagogue was not set up to cater the banquets and lavish Bar Mitzvahs of today, which bring revenue to the temple. At that time, the bar mitzvah boy recited the Haftorah (a reading from the Prophets, followed by a reading from the Torah on Saturday), followed by modest refreshments (usually pickled herring with toothpicks, challah, schnapps) for the congregation.

The Rabbi depended on donations from the congregation who came there to pray on Friday night, Saturday, and the important Jewish holidays, or to say Kaddish (daily prayers for recently departed dear ones). The largest donations arrived around the Jewish New Year: Rosh Hashonah and Yom Kippur.

The 1930's was the time of the Great Depression. Nobody had money. My mother certainly had little money, but she gave as much as she could afford. However, she made it her mission to help the Rabbi and his family.

She organized an all-women fund-raising committee and announced that they were adopting the Rabbi, that it would be a mitzvah (good deed) to help him. The committee enthusiastically arranged luncheons and theater parties. They went to the Jewish theaters of the time: Hopkinson and Parkway Theatres in Brooklyn and the Second Avenue Theatre in New York City.

They would make a deal with the theater manager to get the tickets at a discount and then they would sell the tickets at a profit, which would be given to the Rabbi. I went to all the Jewish shows with my mother on a child's half-price ticket. The Jewish actors were very talented. They sang and danced. They could be comical or very dramatic. They had heart-rending scenes, which brought tears to everyone's eyes. They could also be funny and you would laugh until you cried. I learned a lot about life from them.

One year, the Rabbi was desperate for money, so he called a conference with the committee and suggested that they raffle the solid silver crowns on the Torah as a fund-raiser.

The crowns were a magnificent work of art with engraved silver bells hanging on them. The crowns were placed on top of the carved poles that held the precious Torah. When the Torah was carried through the synagogue on Saturday and certain holidays, the bells tinkled a beautiful tune.

The committee got to work and had raffle books printed with ten raffles in each book. Each raffle cost 50 cents; a whole book of ten raffles would be sold at a discounted price of $4.

I remember my mother sitting at a table near the cashier in Dubrow's Cafeteria on Eastern Parkway, selling raffles to customers as they paid their checks. They used the change from their checks to buy a raffle or two. This was a choice location and my mother was lucky to get it because the Dubrow family were patients of my brother, the doctor, and they were happy to do this favor for him. The other women had different ways of selling the raffles. Sales of the raffles raised a nice amount of money.

Then the day came to pick the raffle out of the hat for the winner of the silver crowns on the Torah. I remember the excitement in the shul (synagogue) as everybody expectantly waited to see who would be the winner.

The Rabbi was appointed to pick the winning raffle out of the hat. You could hear a pin drop as he reached into the hat and called out the number.

Guess who had the winning raffle number? My mother!

There was a murmur of approval as the congregation agreed, "Nobody deserved to win more than my mother because she worked so hard for the Rabbi".

My mother graciously accepted the crowns from the Rabbi and announced that she would take them to display when she made a celebration dinner for her family. Then she would return them to the Rabbi to place back on the Torah. She received a great ovation from the congregation for her generosity and kindness. This was another mitzvah (good deed). I remember helping my mother polish the silver crowns and bells before she returned them to the Rabbi.

Addendum: The last I heard about the Rabbi's blind son was that he became a philosophy professor at one of the great universities in New York.

In retrospect, as a nonagenarian now with the wisdom and knowledge of human nature that come with age, I suspect that it was a put-up job that my mother won the crowns because the

Rabbi did not want to give the crowns to just anybody as a prize. Making my mom the winner would ensure that the crowns would remain in the shul's possession. I may be all wrong in this theory because my mother happened to be a lucky winner. She always seemed to win something when there was something to be won. There are people like that.

29

PREVENTING FORECLOSURE DURING THE DEPRESSION

In the new house on 92 street, my family occupied the first-floor six-room apartment. The two smaller apartments on the second floor were rented to tenants who paid rent.

Deep depression days had arrived and money was very scarce. Families were doubling up because they couldn't afford to pay rent. It was difficult to find tenants for the upstairs apartments. Mom was in charge of the house and was forced to lower the rent or even provide free rent for a month or two as a concession to get the apartments rented.

The mortgage had to be paid and Mom did what she could to keep the house from being foreclosed.

About this time, President Franklin D. Roosevelt established the Home Owners Loan Corporation (HOLC). All the mortgagee had to do was pay the interest on the mortgage every month, and there would not be any foreclosure. My mother signed up and had to pay $50 each month, which she could manage to pay. I remember going to the HOLC office every month with my mom to pay the $50 in cash and get a receipt.

I also remember taking the Pitkin Avenue bus to the Provident Loan Society, which was a sort of pawnshop, where they would lend you money for the jewelry you left with them after they appraised it. If Mom did not have the $50 to bring to the HOLC, she would pawn some of her jewelry and redeem it when she had accumulated enough money. I do not know how she did it, but she avoided foreclosure and got her jewelry back.

I also remember going with her to Empire Gold Buying Company in the Empire State Building. They were located on the second floor, and could be reached with an escalator or elevator. She would use neither the escalator nor elevator. I think she didn't trust them. She insisted on walking up the steps to the second floor. However, the second floor was more than one flight, because the ceiling in the lobby was very high and the second floor was more like the fourth floor. I walked with her and found the offices of Empire Gold Buying.

She was going to sell a platinum bracelet with 82 small diamonds that Pop had given her when one of the children was born. She said she didn't wear it much and the money would help keep the house.

When we entered the office, they were very hospitable, offering us refreshments. A very kindly old gentleman took the bracelet to appraise it. He showed my mom that some diamonds had fallen out and that others looked like the prongs were loose, so it was a good idea to sell it now before more diamonds fell out.

I do not know what Pop had paid for the bracelet twenty-odd years ago when he bought it from Yussel Der Longer on the corner of Delancey Street, but Mom was offered $250 now. She accepted it and we walked down to the lobby.

The bracelet would surely be worth much more today. My mother did what she had to do.

30

CHILDHOOD MEMORIES OF MAKING WINE DURING PROHIBITION

Prohibition was in effect from 1919 until 1933. It was illegal to sell alcoholic beverages, but you were allowed to make wine for private consumption. Being a Romanian, Pop loved his wine and had all the equipment for making it.

Making wine was a family activity in which we all participated.

Sometime in September, Pop would gather the whole family together and drive to Bushwick Avenue, an Italian neighborhood in Brooklyn, where there would be lots of trucks loaded with crates filled with the grape harvest, some dark purple (almost black), some red, some greenish yellow.

Pop would pick certain crates filled with grapes that he thought would make good wine. He would ask me, the youngest (I was maybe 4 or 5 years old), to taste the grapes, which were different from table grapes we buy today. The wine grapes' skin separated from the very juicy flesh very easily and the pits were very big. If I liked the flavor of the grapes, Pop would buy that crate.

The boys would load the car with crates of grapes and then carry them into the basement of our house. Pop would get out all his equipment: a hand-operated wine press, a clean bucket with a lip for pouring, wooden barrels with bungs for sealing the barrels, plus garbage cans to collect the waste.

The hand-cranked wine press separated the skin and pits and sent the grape juice squeezed from the flesh into the clean bucket. Before the grapes could be pressed, we had to remove the stems and leaves. The boys took turns cranking the wine press handle, which was hard work. In the meantime, everybody else was working on removing stems and leaves. The wine press had to be cleaned periodically because the grape skins and seeds clogged it and wouldn't allow the grape juice to flow freely. As the bucket filled up, the grape juice was poured through a funnel into the small opening at the top of the wooden barrel and then sealed with a bung. No sugar was ever added to my father's wine.

As a very little girl, my job was not only to help remove stems and leaves, but to put the 78 rpm records on the hand cranked Victrola, so we could have music while we were making wine. We had Caruso, Melba, Gigli and Lily Pons singing opera. We also had Rudy Vallee and Russ Colombo singing current popular songs of the day on the platters. We knew the words to all the music, so we would all be working and singing and having a wonderful time together! Those were happy times!

When all the barrels were full, and there must have been eight or ten, they would be rolled into the cold storage room in the corner of the basement of our house. This was a room lined with cement blocks and was a bit chilly, even on hot days. The wine would be left to ferment and age for a certain period of time until Pop would call everybody together to taste-test the wine. If the wine was left there too long, it could develop an "essig shtuch" (become acidic). If it had not fermented long enough, it would have a green flavor, and would have to be left in the barrel for a longer period.

There was a spigot near the bottom of the barrel, from which, when turned to open, wine ran into a glass. Pop would pass the glass around for everybody to taste, even to me. We would give our opinions and Pop would then decide whether the wine in that barrel was ready.

If the wine was ready, Pop would fill dark green glass bottles with the wine and cork them with a special corker to get a tight fit. And, voila! We had wine to serve with dinner every night, but especially on Friday nights and holidays.

Wine and beer were served to everybody, including the children. We drank wine and beer to enhance the meal, not to get drunk. Even I, who was much younger than all the other children, was always given a little bit of beer or a wine spritzer (diluted with seltzer) with the meal. Contrary to current dire precautions, we had no alcoholics in the family and nobody's growth was stunted.

31

TELEPHONES, RADIOS IN THE 20'S AND 30'S

In my parents' milieu in the 1920's, just after the end of World War I, very few people owned cars, just as very few had telephones. Pop got a wall-hung telephone (with separate mouthpiece and hand-held receiver) as soon as they were made available.

Harry, of course, needed a telephone for his medical practice. Our neighbors, who did not have telephones, gave our telephone number to friends and relatives. When they received a call, we would call them to our phone. It was a nuisance, but we were friendly neighbors.

If you didn't have a neighbor with a phone, you received calls in the corner candy or drug store phone booth, and one of the kids hanging around would go to your house to tell you of the call, for which you gave him a few pennies as a tip.

Our telephone number was Minnesota 9-4020, which was later changed to Dickens 6-4020. Instead of all numbers, the first two digits were letters in a name. There was no area code. I think that was easier to remember and more fun.

Television was not in existence yet. We bought our first TV in 1950 with antennae like rabbit ears, which had to be adjusted for reception.

In the 30's and 40's we had a Philco radio in a beautiful mahogany cabinet, which was in the dining room. After dinner, we sat around the table noshing as usual, and listening to Jack Benny (who created a character who was a cheapskate) and Eddie Cantor (who sang and talked about his wife, Ida and five daughters), Fred Allen, Fibber McGee and Molly and Joe Penner ("Wanna buy a duck? Quack, quack!), which were all broadcast live.

I particularly liked the mystery programs: "The Inner Sanctum and "The Shadow". We also listened to Major Bowes' Amateur Hour where he hit a very loud bong if the amateur was terrible.

We had a beautifully finished shiny player piano, on which I took lessons for 50 cents an hour. We had a cabinet which stored hundreds of rolls of music for the player part of the piano. To operate the player, you placed the music roll in a compartment at the top of the piano and pushed a lever, which released the pedals so you could pump them with your feet to roll the perforated rolls, which made the music. The words were printed on the rolls. My favorites were "Santa Lucia" and "The Isle of Capri". We all knew the words and would stand around and sing while one of us pumped the pedals.

We were a happy family most of the time. For me, growing up with my wonderful brothers and sister helped me to be the person I am today.

32

TZIPRA'S DOGS

Tzipra (my mom) never met a dog she could not love and make it love her. In the 1930's, during the Great Depression, many people could not afford to feed their pets, so they abandoned them far away from home, hoping they would not find their way back.

Mom felt so sorry when she saw a stray dog jogging in the street, with his tongue hanging out, his tail down with a sad look in his eyes, looking forlorn because it was either lost or abandoned. She would call the dog to her, give it some water and some food, then take it in the house and give it a bath, and guess what? The dog became her loyal, loving companion. We usually had at least one, sometimes two or three dogs at a time.

When it got to four, mom would ask the neighbors if they wanted a nice dog.

Mom's dogs were not allowed on the beds, the couches or the furniture. They knew they had to stay on the floor, which had oriental rugs in the living and dining rooms. At night, they would sleep on the floor next to my mom's bed. If I wanted to get to her, I had to climb over the dogs.

The only prepared dog food available in those days was some kind of canned meat, which she wouldn't bring into the house. Since my mom kept a kosher home, she cooked kosher food for the dogs. The butcher was very kind and gave her the scraps he cut off when trimming the meat.

The dogs loved her food. Only one dog gave her trouble. It was Pal, a fox terrier mix stray, who would sniff the food and turn away. The only food he would eat were broiled chicken livers that my mom fed him with her fingers. She catered to her dogs just as she catered to her family.

Very often, my job was to take the dogs out to an empty lot two blocks away to do their business. (No plastic bags). All three were on leashes and were well behaved. When we got to the empty lot, I took the leashes off and they would run around and play.

The hard part was to get the leashes back on and head for home. They would tease me and make believe they were coming when I called, but run away the last minute. I had to turn my back and pretend that I was leaving without them. Then they would come back for the leash so we could go home.

The first dog I heard about was Peanuts, a stray that my brother Maxie picked up and brought home. Peanuts had puppies once a year, which would be given away to friends and neighbors. Sadly, she died giving birth to her fourth litter the same night I was born, because my mother was busy with her own birth and could not help Peanuts, which she had always done in the past.

The next dog I knew was Beauty, a collie who deserved the name "Beauty", because she was truly beautiful. Beauty was the replacement for Peanuts. I remember her because I remember seeing snapshots of her sitting next to my wicker carriage with me as a baby, sitting in it. She stood guard over me. If anybody came near me, she would snarl and growl.

My brother, Barney brought home a big ugly brown stray that looked something like Little Orphan Annie's dog "Sandy". We thought he was part Airedale. Barney named him "Buck" and they were devoted to each other. When Barney had to leave the house, Buck would lay around looking very sad. As soon as Barney came home, there was joy in the house.

One of the dogs that I remember is Mickey, a Pekingese, whose real name was Pom Pom, the name he had when he was a Blue Ribbon winner in a contest. He had belonged to Harry's wife, Hattie, who got tired of taking care of him. So, my mom took him. Mickey was very tiny and very bossy and had a yip yip bark that astonished the other dogs who were very large.

When my mom put their food out in separate dishes, Mickey would not let the other dogs come near the dishes. It was funny to see this little Pekingese forcing the much bigger dogs to do what he wanted.

When Harry was an intern at Beth-El Hospital, he had to respond to an emergency call at Belmont Race Track. Harry and another intern got into the ambulance with siren blaring.

When they were finished taking care of the emergency, somebody approached them and asked if they wanted a newborn German shepherd puppy that had been born at the track.

Nobody wanted it because it was the runt of the litter, so tiny that nobody believed it would live. Harry was sure Mom would take it so he tucked it into his chest pocket to keep it warm and brought it home. It was so tiny that Mom had to feed it with an eye dropper. We gave him a royal name: Rex. Mom's dogs got a bath every Friday. She had hired a little black man with a crooked back many years ago to clean the house. I remember when he came to the door the first time. It seems that nobody would hire him because of the way he looked. My mother felt sorry for him and said she would let him try one time. It turned out that he did a good job and was honest. His name was Johnny and he worked for my mother for many years.

The last two rooms he cleaned were the kitchen and then the bathroom. When he started cleaning the kitchen, the dogs knew that they would get their bath next before he cleaned the bathroom. They hid under the beds and my mom and I had to poke them out with broomsticks. Mom got all three dogs into the bathroom and soaped and rinsed them in the stall shower.

They accepted the bath with tail down. After the bath, they shook themselves, making a mess in the bathroom. Mom had provided old towels and blankets for them to roll around in to get dry. My job was to brush them. After it was all over, they strutted around showing off how handsome they were. Mom's dogs were fun!

Ordinarily, when Mom picked up a stray, it was usually somebody has abandoned house pet and was already house broken.

Instinctively, however, she knew how to housebreak a dog successfully, which she had to do with Rex who was very intelligent and caught on very quickly. Rex grew into a very large dog, almost the size of a pony. When he barked, the walls shook and when he ran through the house, the floors and the whole house rattled. He was too large a dog to keep in our six-room apartment.

Eventually, Max found a farmer who said he would take the dog. He had a large piece of land in the Catskills, which was a more suitable environment for Rex. We went to visit him many times on the farm.

He wagged his tail furiously in recognition, and jumped all over us. But when we left, he did not look forlorn, which meant that he was happy where he was.

33

WHEN SIXTY CENTS AN HOUR WAS CONSIDERED GOOD PAY

I just ran across a "This Date in History" article I had cut out of Newsday a while ago. The article reads "1914 Auto industrialist Henry Ford announced he was going to pay workers $5 for an 8-hour day, as opposed to $2.34 for a 9-hour day. (Employees still worked six days a week: the 5-day work week was instituted in 1926)."

I remembered why I had clipped the article. First of all, I was born in 1926, (which makes me 90+ now), and I am always interested in anything that happened that year. Secondly, it brought back memories of my paying jobs when I was a teenager in the 1930's and 40's.

When I was almost 14, I started babysitting. The pay was 50 cents for the whole night, usually

Saturday. The one good thing was that after the parents left and the children were asleep, I telephoned three or four of my girl friends to come over and keep me company. We listened to The Hit Parade on the radio (there was no TV) and new dances, like the Lindy and the Cha Cha. One of the girls had started smoking, so the rest of us practiced smoking her cigarettes. There was a lot of coughing and choking when we tried to inhale. None of us became habitual smokers. Today it would probably be cigarettes and pot.

The children usually slept through all this. Before the parents came home, my friends were gone and we had cleaned up all traces of our activities.

I was 15 when World War II started on December 7, 1941. My brother Max enlisted in the army and was a pharmacist on a hospital ship in the Pacific. President Franklin D. Roosevelt was urging everybody to join the war effort. I took his plea seriously. I was in 11ᵗʰ grade at Samuel J. Tilden High School in Brooklyn the summer of 1942. *I* saw a New York Times ad for a job in a defense plant which was paying 60 cents an hour.

Minimum wage at that time was 40 cents an hour. If I worked 40 hours a week at 60 cents an hour, I would earn $24 per week. That appealed to me. I applied for the job and had to produce my birth certificate to prove that I was a U.S.

citizen (because this was a war plant and I had to prove I wasn't a spy). I had to recite and sign a pledge of loyalty to the United States of America. I also had to provide parental-signed working papers because I was underage at 15. I went to the Bureau of Records at 210 Livingston St. in Brooklyn for my birth certificate. My school provided the working papers.

Finally, I was hired to work in a mica plant on Water Street on the waterfront in downtown New York. Subway fare was 5 cents each way.

There was no place to go out for lunch, so I brown-bagged lunch each day.

I was put to work inspecting mica chips. Mica is a rock like asbestos. You have probably seen shiny silvery mica on local rocks. The mica in this factory was delivered in large sheets, which were cut off tall mountainsides in Canada.

At one end of the loft floor were men stamping out certain shapes from the mica sheets with very noisy, deafening stamping machines. The stamping process created dust, which could be seen floating in the air. At the other end of the loft is where I sat at a very large table with 9 other women of all ages. Some of the women worked at this job full time all year.

Sixty cents an hour was considered very good pay. They felt lucky to have this job.

Our job was to inspect the punched-out mica chips (which were in different shapes such as square, round or diamond) to make sure there were no jagged edges. The perfectly shaped mica chips, which did not burn, much like asbestos, were used to fill airplane wings.

I intended to work there for the ten school summer vacation weeks. However, after about eight weeks, some mica dust got in my eye. I had to go to Dr. Cyrus Lack, an ophthalmologist to have it removed. It was hard to remove because it is the same color as the white of the eye and the doctor had a difficult time locating it.

Dr. Lack was a friend of my brother Harry. He asked me if Harry knew that I was working in a mica plant. I told him that I had never mentioned it to him. Dr. Lack told me to tell my brother that he ordered me to quit the job. I did not go back to work after the eye incident.

Since mica is similar to asbestos, I think all those people who worked in that factory must have contracted diseases similar to the 9/11 victims who inhaled asbestos dust. Nobody thought about wearing protective masks or goggles.

I was lucky that I worked there only a few weeks and have no permanent damage to show for it.

That was the end of my teen-age work experience. I felt that I had aided the war effort and had earned some money.

In September I went back to graduate from high school and then on to Brooklyn College where tuition was free. I did need money to pay for books which were not provided by the school. The money I had earned was used to pay the college registration fee, buy used books, and pay for subway fare to get to and from college.

In retrospect, all this was accomplished without a computer, cell phone, iPhone, iPad, or smart phone. I had an old manual Royal typewriter, but I hand-wrote almost everything in legible script.

I spent a lot of time in the college library or the public library on the corner of Eastern Parkway and Schenectady Ave. in Brooklyn. I always made sure I had some nickels with me in case I had to make a telephone call from a phone booth on the street corner. That was my teen-age life in the 30's and 40's.

Lately, there has been talk of increasing the minimum wage from $12 per hour to $15 per hour. Those numbers were beyond my imagination back in the 30's and 40's. But everything is relative. Potatoes were less than one cent per pound back then. Today, potatoes are about 50 cents per pound.

34

WHATEVER HAPPENED TO CHINESE LAUNDRIES?

My husband, Murray and I were in the supermarket on Old Country Road when this beautiful, tall young Chinese woman walked up to my husband and said, "Hello, WN 1". We were startled for the moment until she said questioningly, "Moy's Laundry?"

Of course, this was Mr. Moy's now grown-up daughter who used to redeem our laundry ticket for Murray's beautifully washed and ironed shirts. She used to help out in the store after school. His laundry mark was WN1. When we brought shirts in to be laundered, she would wrap them with a ticket that had a number on it and give us a ticket with the same number, which we would present when we picked up the washed and ironed laundry.

At the supermarket, she confessed that she never knew our name. My husband was always referred to by his laundry mark: WN1.

How did we get such a simple laundry mark? Most laundry marks are a long series of numbers and letters. We had just WN1. In 1948, when we were married, like a dutiful new housewife, I washed and ironed his shirts just once. Murray's sympathetic reaction when he saw them was, "I think we had better bring them to the Chinese laundry." I never washed and ironed his shirts again.

At that time, we were living in a summer bungalow that had been converted to winter use. After World War II, it was hard to find an apartment, so we took this bungalow on Beach 25th Street in Far Rockaway for the winter at a rental of $79 a month. The nine-month rental was low, but the summer rate quadrupled. It was close to the Wavecrest station of the Long Island RR's Far Rockaway Line, which was convenient for us because we both worked in Manhattan and we did not have a car.

Between our bungalow and the railroad was a small strip mall with four shops: a kosher butcher, a grocery store, a dry cleaner and a Chinese laundry. Since all of Murray's shirts were brand new bought by his mom as a sort of trousseau, they had no laundry mark. Thus, his personal laundry mark was created by the Chinese laundry and printed in indelible ink on the back of each collar. W (for Wavecrest), N (our surname), the numeral 1 for the for the first WN. This laundry mark was permanently his. I remember in some old mystery movies, detectives would look for a laundry mark on the clothing of a dead body if there was no other identification.

In 1948, men who worked in an office wore suits with beautifully laundered shirts, ties, polished shoes, sometimes cuff links, a tie clasp and, when they went outdoors, a brimmed felt hat. Murray was a CPA and had clients who manufactured ties, hats, suits and other menswear, so he had to look good when he visited a client because people in the fashion business look you over carefully.

When he walked out of the house in the morning, he looked very professional and band box stylish. Someimes he wore a gray Homburg, which was the style of hat worn by the Prince of Wales (later King Edward VIII, who abdicated the throne). I was very proud of my husband. He was my Prince of Wales.

When we moved to Plainview, we started to use Moy's Laundry. Mr. Moy took care of Murray's shirts until Murray retired in 1990.

Life is different today. Gone are the ironed shirts, ties, cuff links and tie clasps, brimmed hats, and shined shoes. Today, we have synthetic drip dry shirts that come out of the dryer looking ironed (but cannot compare to the cotton shirts washed and ironed by Mr. Moy). Hardly anybody wears a tie. Cuff links and tie clasps have become collector's items. Hats have either disappeared or been replaced by caps or hoodies. Sneakers have replaced shoes; every day is dress down day.

In the old days, when we went to the airport to fly someplace, we got all dressed up. I remember wearing a lovely suit, carefully chosen jewelry, a hat, gloves, high-heeled shoes and a matching handbag. My husband also was dressed meticulously. The stewardesses (now called flight attendants) were perfectly uniformed, coifed and made up. Flying was exciting and romantic. I looked forward to the meal that was served. I always ordered the filet mignon, which was a tiny portion, but always delicious. The flight attendants were very attentive and accommodating. All that has changed. Passengers now wear comfortable clothes, most airlines offer snacks instead of meals, flight attendants seem a little harried and not so attentive and accommodating because they are short-staffed. Airlines do all they can to cut costs, even though the airfares go up. Today an airplane flight is pretty much like a bus or train ride.

I remember how surprised I was when some people came to a matinee performance at the Metropolitan Opera wearing dungarees and sweatshirts. On this particular day, we recognized the great opera star Placido Domingo sitting in the fifth row on the aisle. The dungaree-clad people were seated two rows behind him. I was glad they were behind him, because I felt it was disrespectful to come to the opera dressed that way and Domingo should be spared seeing them.

We had subscribed to the Met for more than 25 years and always dressed up as everybody else did. Going to the opera was a memorable event and part of the enjoyment was seeing some of the "beautiful people" in their minks and sables. As time moved on, I noticed that more and more people dressed down at the opera. I liked it better at the Baths of Caracalla in Rome, where everybody came in evening gowns and tuxedos.The atmosphere was more festive. But maybe the new informality is better.

I also remember when I attended Winthrop Junior High in Brooklyn, a public school. Boys and girls had to wear a white shirt or blouse, red tie, dark skirt for the girls and dark pants for the boys. Girls were not allowed to wear "slacks", as we called them. The school was much disciplined in all ways. We had a high scholastic standing, and I believe it had something to do with the discipline and de-emphasis on clothing. Today, I see young girls carrying expensive designer handbags to school along with their backpacks.

The designer handbag is a status symbol, along with the $80 sneakers.

As an nonagenarian, I don't dress up very often. Most of the time, I am dressed down. I go with the times. Thinking about Mr. Moy's daughter brought back long forgotten memories. Sadly, Murray passed away in 2010 after 62 years of marriage to me. He would have gotten a kick out of hearing me retell the story of his laundry mark.

35

EPILOGUE

As the youngest and last living child of Joseph and Tzipra Samuels' six children, I wrote these memoirs because I felt compelled to tell as much of their story as I can remember, so that their descendants will know their extraordinarily rich history before these memories are lost forever.

This has been a compilation of stories my mother and father told me of their lives in Europe in the 1800's, as well as my personal childhood memories of my family and life in the 20's, 30's and 40's. I am still surprised at how much I remembered.

My family should be aware that we are here because Joseph, my father, walked, worked and hitchhiked 1981 miles from Romania to Hamburg to get on a ship to America. Then he traveled another 4,195 miles across the ocean to America to be the first of the Smilovici's (later Samlowitz's and Samuels') in America. We are all lucky that he had the determination to make THE 6,000 MILE JOURNEY.

ABOUT THE AUTHOR

Rhoda Samuels Nichter is a nonagenarian author-lecturer, who recently retired as a Certified Smoking Cessation Specialist at St. Francis Hospital. She is the author of "How to Stop Smoking Once And For All" and "Yes, I Do Mind If You Smoke!" which were instrumental in obtaining legislation to ban smoking in workplaces, restaurants and all public places. For her efforts, she was honored by the American Lung Association with a "Nonsmokers' Rights Award". She has also been honored with the Albert Nelson Marquis Lifetime Achievement Award.

Walt Whitman said, "There will come a time here in Brooklyn as well as all over America when authentic reminiscences of the past will be of great importance."

The true life stories in "THE SIX THOUSAND MILE JOURNEY" are authentic reminiscences as told by Rhoda Samuels Nichter's parents going back to the late 1800's and her own "fly on the wall" memories of life in the 1920's, 30's and 40's from the age of four on. She was a "little pitcher with big ears" who observed, heard and overheard, and said nothing, but remembered, and now is telling all.

FAMILY ALBUM

Sam, Max and Harry

Barney, Florence, Sam, Max and Harry

Baby Rhoda with Beauty the Collie

Max, Harry, Celia, Baby Sam and Joseph

Made in the USA
Columbia, SC
23 March 2020

89814455R00112